# Notes On Witchcraft

George Lyman Kittredge

# NOTES ON WITCHCRAFT

BY

GEORGE LYMAN KITTREDGE

REPRINTED FROM THE
PROCEEDINGS OF THE AMERICAN ANTIQUARIAN SOCIETY
VOLUME XVIII

WORCESTER, MASSACHUSETTS
THE DAVIS PRESS
1907

33113

# NOTES ON WITCHCRAFT.

BY GEORGE LYMAN KITTREDGE.

We are all specialists now-a-days, I suppose. The good
old times of the polymath and the Doctor Universalis
are gone forever. Yet signs are not wanting that some of
us are alive to the danger of building our party-walls too
high. In one respect, at all events, there can be no doubt
that the investigators of New England antiquities are aware
of their peril, though they occasionally shut their eyes to
it,—I mean, the tendency to consider the Colonists as a
peculiar people, separated from the Mother Country not
only geographically, but also with regard to those currents
of thought and feeling which are the most significant facts
of history. True, there is more or less justification for that
kind of study which looks at the annals of America as ends-
in-themselves; but such study is ticklish business, and it
now and then distorts the perspective in a rather fantastic
way. This is a rank truism. Still, commonplaces are
occasionally steadying to the intellect, and Dr. Johnson—
whose own truths have been characterized by a brilliant
critic as "too true"—knew what he was about when he
said that men usually need not so much to be informed as
to be reminded.

The darkest page of New England history is, by common
consent, that which is inscribed with the words Salem Witchcraft. The hand of the apologist trembles as it turns the
leaf. The reactionary writer who prefers iconoclasm to
hero-worship sharpens his pen and pours fresh gall into his
inkpot when he comes to this sinister subject. Let us try
to consider the matter, for a few minutes, unemotionally,
and to that end let us pass in review a number of facts
which may help us to look at the Witchcraft Delusion of

1692 in its due proportions,—not as an abnormal outbreak of fanaticism, not as an isolated tragedy, but as a mere incident, a brief and transitory episode in the biography of a terrible, but perfectly natural, superstition.

In the first place, we know that the New Englanders did not invent the belief in witchcraft.[1] It is a universally human belief. No race or nation is exempt from it. Formerly, it was an article in the creed of everybody in the world, and it is still held, in some form or other, and to a greater or less extent, by a large majority of mankind.[2]

---

[1] That the New Englanders brought their views on demonology and witchcraft with them from the Mother Country is a self-evident proposition, but it may be worth while to refer to a striking instance of the kind. The Rev. John Higginson, writing from Salem to Increase Mather in 1683, sends him two cases for his Illustrious Providences,—both of which he "believes to be certain." The first is an account of how a mysterious stranger, thought to be the devil, once lent a conjuring book to "godly Mr. [Samuel] Sharp, who was Ruling Elder of the Church of Salem allmost 30 years." The incident took place when Sharp was a young man in London. The second narrative Mr. Higginson "heard at Gilford from a godly old man yet living. He came from Essex, and hath been in N. E. about 50 years." It is a powerfully interesting legend of the Faust type, localised in Essex. In a postscript Mr. Higginson adds, "I had credible information of one in Leicestershire, in the time of the Long Parliament, that gave his soul to the Divel, upon condition to be a Famous Preacher, which he was for a time, &c., but I am imperfect in the story." (Mather Papers, Mass. Hist. Soc. Collections, 4th Series, VIII, 285-287). See also the cases of witchcraft before 1692 collected in S. G. Drake's Annals of Witchcraft in New England. Dr. Poole is far nearer the truth in saying that "the New-England colonists had no views concerning witchcraft and diabolical agency which they did not bring with them from the Old World" (Witchcraft in Boston, in Winsor, Memorial History of Boston, II, 131) than President White is when he remarks that "the life of the early colonists in New England was such as to give rapid growth to the germs of the doctrine of possession brought from the mother country" (Warfare of Science with Theology, II, 145).

[2] A masterly short account of the various elements which made up the fully developed doctrine of witchcraft as it was held during the three centuries of especial prosecution (1400-1700), and of the sources from which these elements were derived, may be found in the first chapter of Joseph Hansen's Zauberwahn, Inquisition und Hexenprozess im Mittelalter (Munich and Leipzig, 1900). A learned and able essay by Professor George L. Burr, The Literature of Witchcraft, reprinted from the Papers of the American Historical Association, New York, 1890, should also be consulted. Professor Burr emphasizes the sound and necessary distinction between witchcraft and magic. But he seems to go too far in his insistence on this distinction as vital in the history of witchcraft: "Magic itself is actual and universal. But witchcraft never was. It was but a shadow, a nightmare: the nightmare of a religion, the shadow of a dogma. Less than five centuries saw its birth, its vigor, its decay" (p. 238; p. 38 of reprint). This statement is true if by witchcraft is meant (and this is Professor Burr's sense) the fully developed and highly complicated system set forth in the Malleus Maleficarum and in Del Rio's Disquisitiones Magicae,—what Hansen (p. 35) calls "der verhängnisvolle Sammelbegriff des Hexenwesens,"—which was not possible until scholasticism had schematised the diversified elements of belief in magic and demonology and sorcery and devil-worship which Christian theology and Christian superstition had derived from the most various sources—

Further, our own attitude of mind toward witchcraft is a very modern attitude indeed. To us, one who asserts the existence, or even the possibility, of the crime of witchcraft staggers under a burden of proof which he cannot conceivably support. His thesis seems to us unreasonable, abnormal, monstrous; it can scarcely be stated in intelligible

---

from Judaism, classical antiquity, Neo-Platonism, and the thousand-and-one beliefs of pagan converts. But, important as this fully developed system was—and true though it may be that without the schematising influence of scholastic philosophy the witch-prosecution which was epidemic in Europe from 1400 to 1700 could hardly have taken place—we should never forget that the essential element in witchcraft is *maleficium*,—the working of harm to the bodies and goods of one's fellow-men by means of evil spirits or of strange powers derived from intercourse with such spirits. This belief in *maleficium* was once universal; it was rooted and grounded in the minds of the people before they became Christians; it is still the creed of most savages and of millions of so-called civilised men. Throughout the history of witchcraft (in whatever sense we understand that word), it remained the ineradicable thing,— the solid foundation, unshakably established in popular belief, for whatever superstructure might be reared by the ingenuity of jurisconsults, philosophers, theologians, or inquisitors. Without this popular belief in *maleficium*, the initial suspicions and complaints which form the basis and starting-point of all prosecutions would have been impossible and inconceivable. *With* this popular belief, the rest was easy. The error into which Professor Burr has fallen is due, no doubt, to his keeping his eye too exclusively on the Continent, where the prosecutions were most extensive, where, in truth, the fully developed system was most prevalent, and where the inquisitorial methods of procedure give to the witch-trials a peculiar air of uniformity and theological schematism. Thus he has been led, like many other historians, to over-emphasize the learned or literary side of the question. For us, however, as the descendants of Englishmen and as students of the history of English colonies in America, it is necessary to fix our attention primarily on the Mother Country. And, if we do this, we cannot fail to perceive that the obstinate belief of the common people in *maleficium*— a belief which, it cannot be too often repeated, is not the work of theologians but the universal and quasi-primitive creed of the human race—is the root of the whole matter. (On savage witchcraft see the anthropologists *passim*. Good examples may be found in Karl von den Steinen, Unter den Naturvölkern Brasiliens, 1894, pp. 339 ff.)

On *maleficium* see especially Hansen, pp. 9 ff. Nothing could be truer than his words:—"Wie viel auch immer im Laufe der Zeit in den Begriff der Zauberei und Hexerei hineingetragen worden ist, so ist doch sein Kern stets das Maleficium geblieben. Aus dieser Vorstellung erwächst die angstvolle Furcht der Menschen und das Verlangen nach gesetzlichem Schutze und blutig strenger Strafe; von ihr hat die strafrechtliche Behandlung dieses Wahns ihren Ausgang genommen" (p. 9). "Das Maleficium, mit Ausnahme des Wettermachens, ist ohne alle Unterbrechung von der kirchlichen und bis in das 17. Jahrhundert auch von der staatlichen Autorität als Realität angenommen, seine Kraft ist nie ernstlich in Abrede gestellt worden; es bildet den roten Faden auch durch die Geschichte der strafrechtlichen Verfolgung" (p. 13). Everybody knows that the most convincing evidence of witchcraft—short of confession or of denunciation by a confederate—was held to be the *damnum minatum* and the *malum secutum*.

The difference between England and the Continent in the development of the witchcraft idea and in the history of prosecution is recognised by Hansen (p. 34, note 1). President White, like Professor Burr, has his eye primarily on the Continent (Warfare of Science with Theology, 1896, I, 350 ff.). His treatment of demoniacal possession, however, is much to our purpose (II, 97 ff., 135 ff.).

6

terms; it savors of madness. Now, before we can do any kind of justice to our forefathers,—a matter, be it remembered, of no moment to them, for they have gone to their reward, but, I take it, of considerable importance to us,— we must empty our heads of all such rationalistic ideas. To the contemporaries of William Stoughton and Samuel Sewall the existence of this crime was not merely an historical phenomenon, it was a fact of contemporary experience. Whoever denied the occurrence of witchcraft in the past, was an atheist; whoever refused to admit its actual possibility in the present, was either stubbornly incredulous, or destitute of the ability to draw an inference. Throughout the seventeenth century, very few persons could be found— not merely in New England, but in the whole world—who would have ventured to take so radical a position. That there had been witches and sorcerers in antiquity was beyond cavil. That there were, or might be, witches and sorcerers in the present was almost equally certain. The crime was recognized by the Bible, by all branches of the Church, by philosophy, by natural science, by the medical faculty, by the law of England. I do not offer these postulates as novelties. They are commonplaces. They will not be attacked by anybody who has even a slight acquaintance with the mass of testimony that might be adduced to establish them.

It is a common practice to ascribe the tenets of the New Englanders in the matter of witchcraft to something peculiar about their religious opinions,—to what is loosely called their Puritan theology. This is a very serious error. The doctrines of our forefathers differed, in this regard, from the doctrines of the Roman and the Anglican Church in no essential,—one may safely add, in no particular. Lord Bacon was not a Puritan,—yet he has left his belief in sorcery recorded in a dozen places. James I. was not a Puritan,[3] but

---

[3] King James's connection with the history of witchcraft almost deserves a monograph, for it has never been adequately discussed, and various misconceptions on the subject are afloat. Thus Mr. H. M. Doughty, in an interesting but one-sided essay on Witchcraft and Christianity (Blackwood's Magazine, March, 1898, CLXIII, 388), remarks that "the new King James had long lived in abject fear of witches" —an assertion that he would find it impossible to prove, even if it were true, as it seems not to be.

his Dæmonologie (1597) is a classic treatise, his zeal in prosecuting sorcerers is notorious, and his statute of 1603[4] was the act under which Matthew Hopkins, in the time of the Commonwealth, sent two hundred witches to the gallows in two years,—nearly ten times as many as perished in Massachusetts from the first settlement to the beginning of the eighteenth century.

Matthew Hopkins, the Witch-Finder General, apparently *was* a Puritan. Indeed, it is his career, more than anything that ever happened in New England, which has led to the reiterated statement that Puritanism was especially favorable, by its temper and its tenets, to prosecution for witchcraft. For his activity falls in the time of the Commonwealth, and the Parliament granted a Special Commission of Oyer and Terminer, in 1645, to try some of the witches that he had detected, and Edmund Calamy was associated with the Commission. But, on the other hand, it must be noted that John Gaule, who opposed Hopkins and is usually credited with most influence in putting an end to his performances, was also a Puritan,—and a minister likewise, and a believer in witches as well. The Hopkins outbreak, as we shall see, must be laid to the disturbed condition of the country rather than to the prevalence of any particular system of theology.[5] Under Cromwell's government, witch trials languished, not because the belief in witchcraft changed, but because there was order once more. So in Scotland,

---

[4] The act of 5 Eliz. c. 16 (after reciting that 33 Henr. VIII. c. 8 had been repealed by 1 Edw. VI. c. 12) prescribes the penalty of death for witchcraft which destroys life, imprisonment for that which causes bodily injury (death for the second offence); in certain harmless kinds of sorcery (such as accompanied the search for treasure or stolen goods) the second offence is punished by imprisonment for life. 1 Jac. I. c. 12 follows 5 Eliz. c. 16 in the main. Its chief differences are,—greater detail in defining witchcraft; the insertion of a passage about digging up dead bodies for purposes of sorcery; death for the first offence in cases of witchcraft which causes bodily injury; death for the second offence in treasure-seeking sorcery and the like. Before one pronounces the new statute much severer than the old, it would be well to examine the practical operation of the two. In particular, one ought to determine how many witches were executed under the law of James I. who would not have been subject to the death penalty under the law of Elisabeth. This is not the place for such an examination. On treasure-seeking sorcery see the learned and entertaining essay of Dr. Augustus Jessopp, Hill-Digging and Magic (in his Random Roaming and Other Papers, 1893).

[5] See p. 64 below. Strictly speaking, the Commonwealth did not begin until 1649, but this point need not be pressed.

8

the conquest by Cromwell checked one of the fiercest prosecutions ever known. The Restoration was followed, both in England and in Scotland, by a marked recrudescence of prosecution.[6]

But we must return to Matthew Hopkins. Let us see how his discoveries affected James Howell. In 1647 Howell writes to Endymion Porter: "We have likewise multitudes of *Witches* among us, for in *Essex* and *Suffolk* there were above two hundred indicted within these two years, and above the one half of them executed: More, I may well say, than ever this Island bred since the Creation, I speak it with horror. God guard us from the Devil, for I think he was never so busy upon any part of the Earth that was enlightned with the beams of *Christianity*; nor do I wonder at it, for there's never a Cross left to fright him away."[7] In the following year, Howell writes to Sir Edward Spencer an elaborate defence of the current tenets in witchcraft and demonology.[8] One striking passage demands quotation:—
"Since the beginning of these unnatural Wars, there may be a cloud of Witnesses produc'd for the proof of this black Tenet: For within the compass of two years, near upon three hundred Witches were arraign'd, and the major part executed in *Essex* and *Suffolk* only. *Scotland* swarms with them now more than ever, and Persons of good Quality executed daily."

It is confidently submitted that nobody will accuse Howell of Puritanism. The letters from which our extracts are taken were written while he was a prisoner in the Fleet

[6] See F. Legge, Witchcraft in Scotland (Scottish Review, XVIII, 267); Thomas Wright, Narratives of Sorcery and Witchcraft, Chap. xxv. Whitelocke, under date of Oct. 4, 1652, notes "Letters that sixty Persons Men and Women were accused before the Commissioners for Administration of Justice in *Scotland* at the last Circuit for Witches; but they found so much Malice and so little Proof against them that none were condemned" (Memorials, 1732, p. 545). Cf. also his very important entry on the same subject under Oct. 29, 1652 (pp. 547–548).

[7] Epistolæ Ho-Elianæ, Familiar Letters, edited by Joseph Jacobs, 1890, book ii, letter 76, p. 506: "To my Honourable Friend, Mr. E. P., at Paris" (cf. Jacobs's notes pp. 783–784). The letter is dated "Fleet, 3 Feb. 1646." This is certainly Old Style. Howell is a queer dater, but a reference in this letter to the departure of the Scottish army (p. 505) proves that the letter was written after Dec. 21, 1646. There is a similar passage about witches in book iii, letter 2, p. 515 (also to Porter), dated "Fleet, 20 Feb. 1646."

[8] Letters, as above, book iii, no. 23, pp. 547 ff., dated "Fleet, 20 Feb. 1647," i. e. doubtless 1648.

under suspicion of being a Royalist spy.[9] His mention of the disappearance of crosses throughout England will not be overlooked by the discriminating reader. It will be noted also that he seems to have perceived a connection—a real one, as we shall see later—[10] between the increase in witchcraft and the turmoil of the Civil War.

Jeremy Taylor was surely no Puritan; but he believed in witchcraft. It is a sin, he tells us, that is "infallibly desperate,"[11] and in his Holy Living (1650) he has even given the weight of his authority to the reality of sexual relations between witches and the devil.[12]

It was not in Puritan times, but in 1664, four years after the Restoration, that Sir Matthew Hale, then Chief Baron of the Exchequer, pronounced from the bench the following opinion in the Bury St. Edmunds case:—' 'That there were such Creatures as *Witches* he made no doubt at all; For *First*, the Scriptures had affirmed so much. *Secondly*, The wisdom of all Nations had provided Laws against such Persons, which is an Argument of their confidence of such a crime. And such hath been the judgment of this Kingdom, as appears by that Act of Parliament[13] which hath provided Punishments proportionable to the quality of the Offence. And desired them [the jury], strictly to observe their Evidence; and desired the great God of Heaven to direct their Hearts in this weighty thing they had in hand: *For to Condemn the Innocent, and to let the Guilty go free, were both an Abomination to the Lord.*"[14] Hale's words were

---

[9] See Jacobs's Introduction, pp. xlii-xliii. The question whether Howell's letters were actually sent to the persons to whom they are addressed or whether they are to be regarded merely as literary exercises composed during his imprisonment (see Jacobs, pp. lxxi ff.) does not affect, for our purposes, the value of the quotations here made, since the letters to which we now refer actually purport to have been written in the Fleet, and since they were first published in the second edition (1650) in the additional third volume and from the nature of things could not have appeared in the first edition (1645). They must, at all events, have been composed before 1650, and are doubtless dated correctly enough.

[10] See p. 64, below.

[11] Sermon xvii (Whole Works, ed. Heber and Eden, 1861, IV, 546).

[12] Whole Works, III, 57; cf. Sermon vii (Works, IV, 412).

[13] See p. 7, above, note 4.

[14] A Tryal of Witches, at the Assizes held at Bury St. Edmonds . . 1664 (London, 1682), pp. 55-56. This report is reprinted in Howell's State Trials, VI, 647 ff., and (in part) in H. L. Stephen's State Trials Political and Social (1899), I, 209 ff. See

fraught with momentous consequences, for he was "allowed on all hands to be the most profound lawyer of his time,"[15] and the Bury case became a precedent of great weight. "It was," writes Cotton Mather, "a Tryal much considered by the Judges of New England."[16]

Hale's conduct on this occasion has of course subjected him to severe criticism. Lord Campbell, for example, goes so far as to declare that he "murdered" the old women,—a dictum which shows but slight comprehension of the temper of the seventeenth century. More creditable to Campbell's historical sense is the following passage:—"Although, at the present day, we regard this trial as a most lamentable exhibition of credulity and inhumanity, I do not know that it at all lowered Hale in public estimation in his own life."[17] Bishop Burnet, as is well-known, makes no mention

---

also Hutchinson, An Historical Essay concerning Witchcraft, chap. viii (1718, pp. 109 ff.; 2d ed., 1720, pp. 139 ff.); Thomas Wright, Narratives of Sorcery and Witchcraft, II., 261 ff. Hale's opinion was regarded as settling the law beyond peradventure. It is quoted, in A True and Impartial Relation of the Informations against Three Witches. . . Assises holden for the County of Devon at the Castle of Exon, Aug. 14, 1682 (London, 1682), Address to the Reader. For Roger North's comments on the Exeter case, see p. 192, below. . A Collection of Modern Relations of Matters of Fact, concerning Witches & Witchcraft, Part I (London, 1693), contains "A Discourse concerning the great Mercy of God, in preserving us from the Power and Malice of Evil Angels. Written by Sir Matt. Hale at Cambridge 26 Mar. 1661. Upon occasion of a Tryal of certain Witches before him the Week before at St. Edmund's Bury." The date is wrong (1661 should be 1664) .but the trial is identified with that which we are considering by the anonymous compiler of the Collection in the following words: "There is a Relation of it in print, written by his Marshal, which I suppose is very true, though to the best of my Memory, not so compleat, as to some observable Circumstances, as what he related to me at his return from that Circuit." The date of the trial is given as "the Tenth day of March, 1664" on the title-page of the report (A Tryal of Witches) and on page 1 as "the Tenth day of March, in the Sixteenth Year of the Reign of . . . Charles II." On page 57 the year is misprinted "1662." Howell's State Trials, VI, 647, 687, makes it 1665, but 16 Charles II. corresponds to Jan. 30, 1664 —Jan. 29, 1665: hence 1664 is right. The (unfinished) Discourse just mentioned must not be confused with Hale's Motives to Watchfulness, in reference to the Good and Evil Angels, which may be found in his Contemplations Moral and Divine, London, 1682 (licensed 1675-6), Part II, pp. 67 ff.

[15] Roger North, Life of the Lord Keeper Guilford, ed. 1826, I, 121.

[16] Wonders of the Invisible World (London, 1693), p. 55. Mather also reproduces the substance of the report above referred to (note 14) in the same work. Bragge, too, reproduces it, in the main, in his tract, Witchcraft Farther Display'd, 1712, in support of the accusation against Jane Wenham.

[17] Lives of the Chief Justices, 1849, I, 561 ff., Chapter xvii. See also the criticism of Hale in a letter of George Onslow's, 1770, 14th Report of the Historical MSS. Commission, Appendix, Part IX, p. 480.

of the case in his Life of Hale.[18]   One might surmise
that he omitted it out of respect for his hero's memory,
since his little book is rather an obituary tribute than a
biography.   More probably, however, Burnet did not regard
the case as any more significant than many other decisions of
Hale's which he likewise passed over in silence.   Unequivocal
evidence that the Bury trial did not injure Hale's reputation
may be found in the silence of Roger North.   North's
elaborate character of Hale, in his Life of the Lord Keeper
Guilford,[19] is notoriously prejudiced in the extreme.
Though admitting Hale's legal learning and many good
qualities, North loses no opportunity to attack his record.
Besides, North praises the Lord Keeper for his conduct in
procuring the acquittal of an alleged witch.   If, then, the
Bury case had seemed to him especially discreditable, or
if he had thought that it afforded an opening for hostile
criticism, we cannot doubt that he would have spoken out
in condemnation.   His complete silence on the subject is
therefore the most emphatic testimony to the general
approval of Hale's proceedings.   Highly significant, too,
is the fact that even Lord Campbell does not blame Hale
for believing in witchcraft, but only for allowing weight to
the evidence in this particular case.   "I would very readily
have pardoned him," he writes, " for an undoubting belief in
witchcraft, and I should have considered that this belief
detracted little from his character for discernment and
humanity.   The Holy Scriptures teach us that, in some ages
of the world, wicked persons, by the agency of evil spirits,
were permitted, through means which exceed the ordinary
powers of nature, to work mischief to their fellow-creatures.
.   .   .   In the reign of Charles II., a judge who from the
bench should have expressed a disbelief in [magic and the
black art] would have been thought to show little respect
for human laws, and to be nothing better than an atheist."
We may profitably compare what Guilford himself (then
Francis North, Chief Justice of the Common Pleas) wrote
of the Devonshire witches in 1682,—nearly twenty years

---

[18] Published in 1682.
[19] Edition of 1826, I, 117 ff.

after the Bury case:—''We cannot reprieve them, without appearing to deny the very being of witches, which, as it is contrary to law, so I think it would be ill for his Majesty's service, for it may give the faction occasion to set afoot the old trade of witch-finding, that may cost many innocent persons their lives which the justice will prevent.''[20]

Sir Thomas Browne, the author of the Religio Medici, was no Puritan, and he was one of the leading scientific men of his day. Yet he gave his opinion, as an expert, at the request of the Court in this same Bury St. Edmunds case, to the following effect:—'That the Devil in such cases did work upon the Bodies of Men and Women, upon a Natural Foundation, (that is) to stir up, and excite such humours super-abounding in their Bodies to a great excess,''[21] and further, that ''he conceived, that these swouning Fits were Natural, and nothing else but what they call the Mother,[22] but only heightned to a great excess by the subtilty of the Devil, co-operating with the Malice of these which we term Witches, at whose Instance he doth these Villanies.''[23]

Browne has been much blamed for this dictum, but there is nothing unreasonable or unscientific in it, if one merely grants the actuality of demoniacal possession, which was then to all intents and purposes an article of faith. If the devil can work upon our bodies at all, of course he can intensify any natural fits or spasms from which we happen to be suffering. Thus Browne's diagnosis of the disease in this case as hysteria, by no means excluded the hypothesis of *maleficium*. But most modern writers refuse to discuss such subjects except *de haut en bas*,—from the vantage-ground of modern science.

Sir Thomas Browne's view was, it seems, substantially identical with that of his predecessor, the famous Robert Burton,—no Puritan either!—who has a whole subsection

---

[20] State Papers (Domestic), 1682, Aug. 19, bundle 427, no. 67, as quoted by Pike. History of Crime in England, II, 238.

[21] A Tryal of Witches, as above, p. 41.

[22] That is, *hysteria*.

[23] A Tryal, as above, p. 42. Cf. the Supplementary Memoir, in Simon Wilkin's edition of Browne's Works, 1852, I, liv-lvi.

"Of Witches and Magitians, how they cause Melancholy," asserting that what "they can doe, is as much almost as the Diuell himselfe, who is still ready to satisfie their desires, to oblige them the more vnto him."[24]

Joseph Glanvill, the author of The Vanity of Dogmatizing, was no Puritan,[25] but a skeptical philosopher, a Fellow of the Royal Society, and Chaplain in Ordinary to King Charles II.; neither was his friend, Dr. Henry More, the most celebrated of the Cambridge Platonists. Yet these two scholars and latitudinarians joined forces to produce that extraordinary treatise, Saducismus Triumphatus: or, A Full and Plain Evidence concerning Witches and Apparitions. This book, an enlarged form of Glanvill's Philosophical Considerations concerning Witchcraft (1666), was published in 1681, and went through no less than five editions, the last appearing as late as 1726.[26] It was thought to have put the belief in apparitions and witchcraft on an unshakable basis of science and philosophy.[27] No English work on the subject had a more powerful influence. When the Rev. John Hale, of Beverley, wrote his Modest Enquiry,[28] which deplored the Salem excesses and protested against spectral evidence,—a notable treatise, published, with a prefatory epistle from the venerable Higginson,[29] in 1702,—he was able to condense the affirm-

---

[24] Anatomy of Melancholy, 1621, Part 1, section 2, member 1, subsection 3. I quote from the edition of 1624.

[25] The following short character of Glanvill, by Bishop Kennet, may be quoted, not because it is just, but because it might conceivably be brought forward by somebody in rebuttal of this proposition:—"Mr. *Joseph Glanvill* of *Lincoln* College, *Oxon*. Taking the Degree of M. A. in the beginning of 1658, was about that Time made Chaplain to old *Francis Rous*, one of *Oliver's* Lords, and Provost of *Eaton* College.— He became a great Admirer of Mr. *Richard Baxter*, and a zealous Person for a Commonwealth. After his Majesty's Restauration he turn'd about, became a Latitudinarian, —Rector of *Bath*, Prebendary of *Worcester*, and Chaplain to the King" (White Kennet, An Historical Register, 1744, p. 931).

[26] See Dr. Ferris Greenslet's Joseph Glanvill, A Study in English Thought and Letters of the Seventeenth Century, New York, 1900, especially Chap. vi. For a bibliography of Glanvill, see Emanuel Green, Bibliotheca Somersetensis, Taunton (Eng.), 1902, I, 206 ff.

[27] More's theories on the subject of apparitions, demons, and witches may also be read, at considerable length, in his Antidote against Atheism, Book iii, Chaps. 2-13 (Philosophical Writings, 2d ed., 1662, pp. 89 ff.); cf. the Appendix to the Antidote, Chaps. 12-13 (pp. 181 ff.) and The Immortality of the Soul, Chap. 16 (pp. 129 ff.).

[28] A Modest Enquiry into the Nature of Witchcraft, Boston, 1702.

[29] Dated 1697-8.

ative part of his argument, because, as he himself says, Glanvill "hath strongly proved the being of Witches."[30]

Dr. Meric Casaubon, Prebend of Canterbury, was not a
Puritan; yet the second part of his Credulity and Incredulity
(1668) contains a vigorous assertion of demonology and
witch-lore, and was republished in 1672 under the alluring
title, A Treatise Proving Spirits, Witches and Supernatural
Operations by Pregnant Instances and Evidences.[31]

Ralph Cudworth, the antagonist of Hobbes, was not a
Puritan. Yet in his great Intellectual System he declares
for the existence of sorcery, and even admits a distinction
between its higher operations—as in the θεουργία of Apol-
lonius of Tyana[32]—and the vulgar performances of everyday
wizards.[33] There is some reason, too, for supposing that
Cudworth took part with Henry More in examining certain
witches at Cambridge, and heard one of them try to recite
the Creed and the Lord's Prayer, as she had offered to do
"as an argument she was no witch."[34]

---

[30] P. 12.

[31] Meric Casaubon was born in 1599 and died in 1671. His learned, lively, and
vastly entertaining work, A Treatise concerning Enthusiasme, as it is an Effect of
Nature: but is mistaken by many for either Divine Inspiration, or Diabolicall Possession, appeared in 1655, and in a "Second edition: revised, and enlarged" in 1656.
It shows an open mind and a temper rather skeptical than credulous. Passages
of interest in our present discussion may be found on pp. 37-41, 44, 49, 94-95, 100,
118, 174 (Quakers), 286, of the second edition. Of particular significance is the Doctor's
account of his visit to a man who was thought to be possessed but whom he believed
to be suffering from some bodily distemper (pp. 97 ff.). Casaubon's treatise (in
two parts) Of Credulity and Incredulity, in Things Natural, Civil, and Divine, came
out in 1668, and was reissued, with a new title-page (as above), in 1672. A third
part, Of Credulity and Incredulity in Things Divine and Spiritual, appeared in 1670.
Webster's assault upon Casaubon in his Displaying of Supposed Witchcraft was
made in apparent ignorance of the fact that the venerable scholar had been dead
for some years (see p. 24, below).

[32] Compare Reginald Scot's chapter "Of Theurgie, with a Confutation thereof"
(Discoverie of Witchcraft, book xv, chap. 42, 1584, p. 466, ed. 1665, p. 280). See
also Henry Hallywell, Melampronoea: or A Discourse of the Polity and Kingdom of
Darkness. Together with a Solution of the Chiefest Objections brought against
the Being of Witches, 1681, pp. 50-51.

[33] Cap. iv, §15, ed. Mosheim, 1773, I, 395-396.

[34] Sadducismus Triumphatus, ed. 1726, p. 336; see James Crossley's Introduction
to Potts, Discovery of Witches in the County of Lancaster, reprinted from the Edition of 1613 (Chetham Society, 1845), p. vi, note 2. This experiment was twice
tried as late as 1712, in the case of Jane Wenham, by the Rev. Mr. Strutt, once in
the presence of Sir Henry Chauncy, and again in the presence of the Rev. Mr. Gardi-
ner. Its ill success is recorded by a third Anglican clergyman,—Mr. Francis Bragge
(A Full and Impartial Account of the Discovery of Sorcery and Witchcraft, Practis'd
by Jane Wenham, London, 1712, pp. 11, 15).

Robert Boyle, the improver of the air-pump and the discoverer of Boyle's Law, had "particular and considerable advantages to persuade [him], upon good grounds" that some witch stories are true, and he thought that Glanvill's investigations would do "a good service to religion."[85] This was in 1677. In the following year Boyle declared his belief[86] in the performances of the devil of Mascon.[87] Boyle's religious views did not hinder him from being a leader in that fervor of scientific experimentation which is one of the glories of the latter half of the seventeenth century. And he too was not a Puritan.

Isaac Barrow, the master of Newton, was not a Puritan. Yet he left on record, in one of his sermons, one of the most powerful and eloquent of all protests against disbelief in the kind of phenomena which our ancestors are so often attacked for crediting. The passage is long, but must be quoted in full, for every word is of weight:—

"I may adjoin to the former sorts of extraordinary actions, some other sorts, the consideration of which (although not so directly and immediately) may serve our main design; those (which the general opinion of mankind hath approved, and manifold testimony hath declared frequently to happen) which concern apparitions from another world, as it were, of beings unusual; concerning spirits haunting persons and places, (these discerned by all senses, and by divers kinds of effects;) of which the old world (the ancient poets and historians) did speak so much, and of which all ages have afforded several attestations very direct and plain, and having all advantages imaginable to beget credence; concerning visions made unto persons of especial eminency and influence, (to priests and prophets;) concerning presignifications of future events by dreams; concerning the power of enchantments, implying the cooperation of invisible powers; concerning all sorts of intercourse and confederacy (formal or virtual) with bad spirits: all which

---

[85] Letter to Glanvill, Sept. 18, 1677, Works, ed. Birch, V, 244. Compare Dr. Samuel Collins's letter to Boyle, Sept. 1, 1663 (Boyle's Works, V, 633-634).

[86] In a letter to Glanvill (Works, V, 245).

[87] See Demonologie ou Traitte des Demons et Sorciers . . . Par Fr. Perreaud. Ensemble l'Antidemon de Mascon, ou Histoire Veritable de ce qu'un Demon a fait & dit, il y a quelques années, en la maison dudit S'. Perreaud à Mascon. Geneva, 1653.

things he that shall affirm to be mere fiction and delusion, must thereby with exceeding immodesty and rudeness charge the world with extreme both vanity and malignity; many, if not all, worthy historians, of much inconsiderateness or fraud; most lawgivers, of great silliness and rashness; most judicatories, of high stupidity or cruelty; a vast number of witnesses, of the greatest malice or madness; all which concurred to assert these matters of fact.

"It is true, no question, but there have been many vain pretences, many false reports, many unjust accusations, and some undue decisions concerning these matters; that the vulgar sort is apt enough to be abused about them; that even intelligent and considerate men may at a distance in regard to some of them be imposed upon; but, as there would be no false gems obtruded, if there were no true ones found in nature; as no counterfeit coin would appear, were there no true one current; so neither can we well suppose that a confidence in some to feign, or a readiness in most to believe, stories of this kind could arise, or should subsist, without some real ground, or without such things having in gross somewhat of truth and reality. However, that the wiser and more refined sort of men, highest in parts and improvements both from study and experience, (indeed the flower of every commonwealth; statesmen, lawgivers, judges, and priests,) upon so many occasions of great importance, after most deliberate scanning such pretences and reports, should so often suffer themselves to be deluded, to the extreme injury of particular persons concerned, to the common abusing of mankind, to the hazard of their own reputation in point of wisdom and honesty, seems nowise reasonable to conceive. In likelihood rather the whole kind of all these things, were it altogether vain and groundless, would upon so frequent and so mature discussions have appeared to be so, and would consequently long since have been disowned, exploded, and thrust out of the world; for, as upon this occasion it is said in Tully, 'Time wipeth out groundless conceits, but confirms that which is founded in nature, and real.'

"Now if the truth and reality of these things, (all or any of them,) inferring the existence of powers invisible, at least inferior ones, though much superior to us in all sort of ability, be admitted, it will at least (as removing the chief obstacles of incredulity) confer much to the belief of that supreme Divinity, which our Discourse strives to maintain.[38]

Dr. George Hickes, of Thesaurus fame, was one of the most eminent scholars of his time. He was also a Non-juror, and titular Bishop of Thetford. In other words, he was not a Puritan. Yet in 1678 Hickes published an account of the infamous Major Weir, the most celebrated of all Scottish wizards, which betrays no skepticism on the cardinal points of sorcery.[39] There is also an extremely interesting letter from the Doctor to Mr. Pepys, dated June 19, 1700, which indicates a belief in witchcraft and second sight. The most curious part of this letter, however, deals with Elf Arrows. "I have another strange story," writes Dr. Hickes, "but very well attested, of an Elf arrow, that was shot at a venerable Irish Bishop by an Evil Spirit in a terrible noise, louder than thunder, which shaked the house where the Bishop was; but this I reserve for his son to tell you, who is one of the deprived Irish Clergymen, and very well known, as by other excellent pieces, so by his late book, entitled, 'The Snake in the Grass.' "[40] What would the critics say if this passage were found in a work of Cotton Mather's?

Finally, it is not amiss to remember that the tolerant, moderate, and scholarly John Evelyn, whom nobody will accuse of being a Puritan, made the following entry in his Diary under February 3d, 1692-3:—''Unheard-of stories of the universal increase of Witches in New England; men, women and children devoting themselves to the devil, so as to threaten the subversion of the government. At the same time there was a conspiracy amongst the negroes in Barbadoes to murder all their masters, discovered by overhearing a discourse of two of the slaves, and so preventing the execution of the designe.'' There is no indication

---

[38] Theological Works, ed. 1830, IV, 480-482.
[39] In his Ravillac Redivivus, reprinted in the Somers Tracts, 2d ed., VIII, 510 ff. (see especially pp. 546 ff.). Weir, who was unquestionably insane, was executed in 1670.
[40] Diary and Correspondence of Samuel Pepys, London, 1885, IV, 275. On elf-arrows cf. Pitcairn, Criminal Trials in Scotland, I, ii, 192, 198; III, 607, 609, 615; W. Henderson, Notes on the Folk-Lore of the Northern Counties, 1879, pp. 185 ff.

that Evelyn regarded either of these conspiracies as less possible of occurrence than the other.[41]

Most of these passages are sufficiently well known, and their significance in the abstract is cheerfully granted, I suppose, by everybody. But the cumulative effect of so much testimony from non-Puritans is, I fear, now and then disregarded or overlooked by writers who concern themselves principally with the annals of New England. Yet the bearing of the evidence is plain enough. The Salem outbreak was not due to Puritanism; it is not assignable to any peculiar temper on the part of our New England ancestors; it is no sign of exceptional bigotry or abnormal superstition. Our forefathers believed in witchcraft, not because they were Puritans, not because they were Colonials, not because they were New Englanders,—but because they were men of their time. They shared the feelings and beliefs of the best hearts and wisest heads of the seventeenth century. What more can be asked of them?[42]

I am well aware that there are a few distinguished names that are always entered on the other side of the account, and some of them we must now consider. It would be unpardonable to detract in any maner from the dear-bought fame of such forerunners of a better dispensation. But we must not forget that they were forerunners. They occupy a much more conspicuous place in modern books than they occupied in the minds of their contemporaries.[43] Further, if we listen closely to the words of these voices in the wilderness, we shall find that they do not sound in unison, and that their testimony is not in all cases precisely what

---

[41] Evelyn may have derived his information from Sir William Phips's letter to the home government (Oct. 14, 1692), as Dr. G. H. Moore suggests (Final Notes on Witchcraft in Massachusetts, N. Y., 1885, p. 66). For the letter see Goodell, Essex Institute Collections, 2d Series, I, ii, 86 ff. Phips's second letter (Feb. 21, 1692-3, to the Earl of Nottingham) is printed by Moore, pp. 90 ff.

[42] The remark, sometimes heard, that Calvinism was especially responsible for witch trials is a loose assertion which has to reckon with the fact that the last burning for witchcraft at Geneva took place in 1652 (see Paul Ladame, Procès criminel de la dernière Sorcière brulée à Genève, Paris, 1888).

[43] Compare Burton, Anatomy of Melancholy, Part I, section 2, member 1, subsection 3:—"Many deny Witches at all, or if there be any, they can doe no harme: of this opinion is Wierus, lib. 3. cap. 53, de prǽstig. dæm. Austin Lerchemer, a Dutch writer, Biarmanus, Ewichius, Euwaldus, our countryman Scot. . . but on the contrary are most Lawyers, Diuines, Physitians, Philosophers."

we should infer from the loose statements often made about them.

Johann Wier, or Weyer (1515-1588), deserves all the honor he has ever received. He devoted years to the study of demonology, and brought his great learning, and his vast experience as a physician, to bear on the elucidation of the whole matter.[44] He held that many of the performances generally ascribed to devils and witches were impossible, and that the witches themselves were deluded. But there is another side to the picture. Wier's book is crammed full of what we should now-a-days regard as the grossest superstition. He credited Satan and his attendant demons with extensive powers. He believed that the fits of the so-called bewitched persons were due in large part to demoniacal possession or obsession, and that the witches themselves, though innocent of what was alleged against them, were in many cases under the influence of the devil, who made them think that they had entered into infernal compacts, and ridden through the air on broomsticks, and killed their neighbors' pigs, and caused disease or death by occult means. And further, he was convinced that such persons as Faust, whom he called *magi*, were acquainted with strange and damnable arts, and that they were worthy of death and their books of the fire. One example may serve to show the world-wide difference between Wier's mental attitude and our own.

One of the best known symptoms of bewitchment was the vomiting of bones, nails, needles, balls of wool, bunches of hair, and other things, some of which were so large that they could not have passed through the throat by any natural means.[45] · Such phenomena, Wier tells us, he had himself seen. How were they to be explained? Easily, according to Wier's general theory. Such articles, he says,

---

[44] Wier's great work, De Praestigiis Daemonum, was published in 1563, and was afterwards much enlarged. It went through many editions.

[45] See the extraordinary list in William Drage, Daimonomageia. A Small Treatise of Sicknesses and Diseases from Witchcraft, and Supernatural Causes, 1665. Webster considers this subject at length in Chap. xii of his Displaying of Supposed Witchcraft, 1677, with a full discussion of van Helmont's views. Cf. Henry More, Antidote against Atheism, Chaps. 4-5 (Philosophical Writings, 2d ed., 1662, pp. 97 ff.).

are put into the patient's mouth by the devil, one after another, as fast as they come out. We cannot see him do this,—either because he acts so rapidly that his motions are invisible, or because he fascinates our sight, or because he darkens our eyes, perhaps by interposing between them and the patient some aërial body.[46]

The instability of Wier's position should not be brought against him as a reproach, since he was far in advance of his contemporaries, and since his arguments against the witch dogma are the foundation of all subsequent skepticism on the subject.[47] Besides, it is certain that such a thoroughgoing denial of the devil's power as Bekker made a century later would have utterly discredited Wier's book and might even have prevented it from being published at all.[48] Yet, when all is said and done, it must be admitted that Wier's doctrines have a half-hearted appearance, and that they seemed to most seventeenth-century scholars to labor under a gross inconsistency. This inconsistency was emphasized by Meric Casaubon. "As for them," writes Dr. Casaubon, "who allow and acknowledge *supernatural operations* by Devils and Spirits, as *Wierius;* who tells as many strange stories of them, and as *incredible*, as are to be found in any book; but stick at the business of *Witches* only, whom they would not have thought the Authors of those mischiefs, that are usually laid to their charge, but the Devil only; though this opinion may seem to some, to have more of *charity*, than *Incredulity;* yet the contrary will easily appear to them, that shall look into it more carefully." And Casaubon dwells upon the fact that Wier grants "no small part of what we drive at, when he doth acknowledge *supernatural operations*, by Devils and Spirits."[49] Indeed, the apparent contradiction in Wier's theories may also excuse

---

[46] "Ea dæmonis subtilitate uelocitateque imperceptibili, ori ingesta, nostris ad hæc oculis uel celeritate eius uictis, uel fascino delusis, uel interiecto corpore aereo aut aliter motis eo intus uel foris uel utrinque humoribus aut spiritu caligantibus." De Præstigiis Dæmonum (Basileæ, 1568), iv, 2, pp. 352-353.

[47] Even Bekker (see p. 35, below), who approaches the subject from the philosophical direction, and whose logical process is different from Wier's, is greatly indebted to him.

[48] Compare the fate of Bekker in 1692 (p. 39).

[49] A Treatise proving Spirits, Witches and Supernatural Operations, 1672, p. 35.

Casaubon for the suggestion he makes that Wier's intention "was not so much to favour *women*, as the *Devil* himself, with whom, it is to be feared, that he was too well acquainted."[50] This reminds us of what King James had already written of "Wierus, a German Physition," who "sets out a publike Apologie for all these craftes-folkes, whereby, procuring for their impunitie, he plainely bewrayes himselfe to have bene one of that profession."[51]

Reginald Scot's Discoverie of Witchcraft appeared in 1584. Scot, who was largely indebted to Wier, goes much farther than his Continental predecessor. Of course he does not deny the existence of evil spirits,[52] but he does not believe, like Wier, that evil spirits are continually occupied in deluding mankind by all manner of false (or præstigious) appearances. Such deceits he ascribes to juggling, and he accordingly gives elaborate directions for the performance of various tricks of legerdemain.[53]

There seems to be a more or less prevalent impression that Scot's book explodes witchcraft so thoroughly that the whole delusion might soon have come to an end in England if James I. had not mounted the throne a short time after it was published. True, King James's Dæmonologie is expressly directed "against the damnable opinions" of Wier and Scot.[54] But, to tell the truth, Scot's treatise

---

[50] The same, p. 46.

[51] Dæmonologie, Workes, 1616, p. 92. On Wier in general, see Carl Binz, Doctor Johann Weyer, ein rheinischer Arzt, der erste Bekämpfer des Hexenwahns, Berlin, 1896.

[52] He expressly asserts his belief in their existence (A Discourse upon Divels and Spirits, chap. 32, p. 540; cf. chap. 16, p. 514).

[53] Discoverie of Witchcraft, xiii, 22-34, ed. 1584, pp. 321 ff., ed. 1665, pp. 181-201 (with cuts). Most of the tricks which Scot describes are identical with feats of legerdemain that are the stock in trade of every modern juggler:—"To throwe a peece of monie awaie, and to find it againe where you list" (p. 326); "To make a groat or a testor to sinke through a table, and to vanish out of a handkercher very strangelie" (p. 327); "How to deliver out foure aces, and to convert them into foure knaves" (p. 333); "To tell one without confederacie what card he thinketh" (p. 334); "To burne a thred, and to make it whole againe with the ashes thereof" (p. 341); "To cut off ones head, and to laie it in a platter, &c.: which the jugglers call the decollation of John Baptist" (p. 349). The picture of the apparatus required for the last-mentioned trick is very curious indeed (p. 353). The references to Scot, unless the contrary is stated, are to all the pages of the first (1584) edition, as reprinted by Dr. Brinsley Nicholson (London, 1886).

[54] King James remarks, in the Preface to his Dæmonologie, that Scot "is not ashamed in publike Print to deny, that there can be such a thing as Witch-craft: and so maintaines the old errour of the Sadduces in denying of spirits" (Workes, 1616, pp. 91-92).

did not require a royal refutation. To us moderns, who
are converted already and need no repentance, its general
air of reasonableness, together with its humor and the
raciness of the style, makes the Discoverie seem convincing
enough. But this is to look at the matter from a mistaken
point of view. The question is, not how Scot's arguments
affect us, but how they were likely to affect his contemporaries.
Now, if the truth must be told, the Discoverie is deficient
in one very important respect. It makes no satisfactory
answer to the insistent questions: "What are these evil
spirits of which the Bible and the philosophers tell us,
and which everybody believes in, and always has believed
in, from the beginning of time? And what are they about?
If they are powerful and malignant, why is it not likely
that the effects which everybody ascribes to them are really
their work? And if they are eager not only to torment
but to seduce mankind, why is it not reasonable to suppose
that they accomplish both ends at the same time—kill
two birds with one stone—by procuring such evil effects
by means of witches, or by allowing themselves to be
utilized by witches as instruments of malice?" It was
quite proper to ask these questions of Scot. He admitted the
existence of evil spirits, but declared that we know little
or nothing about them, denied that they can produce the
phenomena then generally ascribed to their agency, and
alleged fraud and delusion to account for such phenomena.
Even to us, with our extraordinary and very modern
incredulity toward supernatural occurrences, the lacuna
in Scot's reasoning is clear enough if we only look at his
argument as a whole. This we are not inclined to do; at
least, no historian of witchcraft has ever done it. It is
easier and more natural for us to accept such portions of
Scot's argument as agree with our own view, to compliment
him for his perspicacity, and to pass on, disregarding the
inadequacy of what he says about evil spirits. Or, if we
notice that his utterances on this topic are halting and
uncertain, we are tempted to regard such hesitancy as
further evidence of his rational temper. He could not
quite deny the existence of devils, we feel,—that would

have been too much to expect of him; but he waves them aside like a sensible man.[55] A moment's consideration, however, will show us that this defect in Scot's case, trifling as it appears to us now-a-days, was in fact a very serious thing. To us, who never think of admitting the intervention of evil spirits in the affairs of this world, the question whether there are any such spirits at all has a purely theoretical interest. Indeed, we practically deny their existence when we ignore them as we do: *de non apparentibus et non existentibus eadem est lex*.—But to Scot's contemporaries, the question of the existence of evil spirits involved the whole matter in debate,—and Scot granted their existence.

A curious particular in the history of Scot's Discoverie should also be considered in estimating its effect on the seventeenth century. The appearance of a new edition in 1665, shortly after the famous Bury St. Edmunds case,[56] may at first sight seem to indicate powerful and continuing influence on the part of the Discoverie. When we observe from the title-page, however, that the publisher has inserted nine chapters at the beginning of Book xv, and has added a second book to the Treatise on Divels and Spirits, our curiosity is excited. Investigation soon shows that these additions were calculated to destroy or minimize the total effect of Scot's book. The prefixed chapters contain directions for making magical circles, for calling up "the ghost of one that hath hanged himself," and for raising various orders of spirits. These chapters are thrust in without any attempt to indicate that they are not consistent with Scot's general plan and his theories. They appear to be, and are, practical directions for magic and necromancy. The additional book is even more dangerous to Scot's design. It is prefaced by the remark:—' 'Because the Author in his foregoing Treatise, upon the *Nature of Spirits and Devils*, hath only touched the subject thereof superficially, omitting the more material part; and with a brief and cursory Tractat,

---

[55] In what an orderly way one may proceed from an admission of the doctrine of fallen angels to the final results of the witch dogma may be seen, for instance, in Henry Hallywell's Melampronoea: or A Discourse of the Polity and Kingdom of Darkness, 1681. Hallywell had been a Fellow of Christ's College, Cambridge.

[56] See p. 9, above.

hath concluded to speak the least of this subject which indeed requires most amply to be illustrated; therefore I thought fit to adjoyn this subsequent discourse; as succedaneous to the fore-going, and conducing to the compleating of the whole work."[57]

How far "this subsequent discourse" is really fitted to complete Scot's work may be judged by a statement which it makes on the very first page, to the effect that bad spirits "are the grand Instigators, stirring up mans heart to attempt the inquiry after the darkest, and most mysterious part of Magick, or Witchcraft." And again a little later:—"Great is the villany of Necromancers, and wicked Magicians, in dealing with the spirits of men departed; whom they invocate, with certain forms, and conjurations, digging up their Carkasses again, or by the help of Sacrifices, and Oblations to the infernal Gods; compelling the Ghost to present it self before them."[58] All this is quite opposed to Scot's view and the whole intention of his book. The insertion of such worthless matter was, of course, a mere trick of the bookseller to make a new edition go off well. But the fact of its insertion shows that Scot was thought to have left his treatise incomplete or unsatisfactory in a most important point. And the inserted matter itself must have gone far to neutralize the effect of republication in a witch-haunted period. And so we may leave Reginald Scot, with our respect for his courage and common sense undiminished, but with a clear idea of the slight effect which his treatise must have had on the tone and temper of the age that we are studying.

John Webster's Displaying of Supposed Witchcraft, which appeared in 1677—the Preface is dated "February 23. 1673"—was particularly directed against Glanvill and Meric Casaubon. It holds a distinguished place in the history of witchcraft, and demands our careful scrutiny. What is usually thought of it has been eloquently expressed by the late Mr. James Crossley. "In this memorable book," writes Mr. Crossley, "he exhausts the subject, as far as

---

[57] P. 39. See Nicholson's reprint of the 1584 edition, p. xlii.
[58] Page 46.

it is possible to do so, by powerful ridicule, cogent arguments, and the most varied and well applied learning, leaving to [Francis] Hutchinson, and others who have since followed in his track, little further necessary than to reproduce his facts and reasonings in a more popular, it can scarcely be said, in a more effective form."[59]

A few of Webster's opinions must be specified, that the reader may judge how far The Displaying of Supposed Witchcraft deserves to rank as a work of sober and scientific reason, and to what extent the author merits the position that seems to be traditionally assigned to him as an uncompromising assailant of superstition.

Angels, good and bad, are "really and truly corporeal" and not spirits, except "in a relative and respective" sense.[60] Since devils are corporeal, Webster admits that "they may move and agitate other bodies." Their strength, however, is limited, "for though one Devil may be supposed to move or lift up that which would load an Horse, yet it will not follow that he can move or lift up as much as would load a Ship of a thousand Tun."[61] Webster grants that "God doth make use of evil Angels to punish the wicked, and to chastise and afflict the godly, and in the effecting of these things that they have a power given them to hurt the earth and the Sea and things therein, as to bring tempests, thunder, lightning, plague, death, drought and the like."[62]

Webster has a profound belief in apparitions and tells some capital ghost stories[63]—'unquestionable testimonies," he calls them, "either from our own Annals, or matters of fact that we know to be true of our own certain knowledge, that thereby it may undoubtedly appear, that there are effects that exceed the ordinary power of natural causes, and may for ever convince all Atheisticall minds."[64] One of

[59] Introduction to the Chetham Society reprint of Potts's Discoverie of Witches, pp. xxxviii–xxxix.
[60] Pages 202–215.
[61] P. 228. Perhaps Webster is merely "putting a case" here; but he certainly seems to be making an admission, at least in theory.
[62] Page 230.
[63] Pages 294 ff.
[64] Page 294.

these tales concerns the murder of one Fletcher by Ralph
Raynard, an innkeeper, and Mark Dunn, a hired assassin.
One day "the spirit of *Fletcher* in his usual shape and habit
did appear unto [Raynard], and said, Oh *Raph*, repent,
repent, for my revenge is at hand." The result was a
full confession. "I have recited this story punctually,"
writes Webster, "as a thing that hath been very much
fixed in my memory, being then but young, and as a
certain truth, I being (with many more) an ear-
witness of their confessions and an eye-witness of their
Executions, and likewise saw *Fletcher* when he was taken
up, where they had buried him in his cloaths, which were
a green fustian doublet pinkt upon white, gray breeches,
and his walking boots and brass spurrs without rowels."
The spectre, Webster is convinced, was an "extrinsick
apparition to *Raynard*," and not the mere effect of a guilty
conscience "which represented the shape of *Fletcher* in
his fancy." The thing could not, he thinks, "be brought
to pass either by the Devil, or *Fletchers* Soul," and therefore he "concludes that either it was wrought by the Divine
Power,...or that it was the Astral or Sydereal Spirit of
*Fletcher*, seeking revenge for the murther."[65]

Webster also believes fully in the "bleeding or cruentation
of the bodies of those that have been murthered," particularly at the touch of the murderer or in his presence,
and he gives a very curious collection of examples, in some
of which "the murtherers had not been certainly known
but by the bleeding of the body murthered."[66] The most
probable explanation of such phenomena he finds in the
existence of the astral spirit, "that, being a middle substance,
betwixt the Soul and the Body doth, when separated from
the Body, wander or hover near about it, bearing with it
the irascible and concupiscible faculties, wherewith being
stirred up to hatred and revenge, it causeth that ebullition
and motion in the blood, that exudation of blood upon
the weapon, and those other wonderful motions of the
Body, Hands, Nostrils and Lips, thereby to discover the

[65] Pages 297-298.
[66] Pages 302-310.

murtherer, and bring him to condign. punishment."[67]
In some cases, however, Webster holds that the soul
has not actually departed, "and God may in his just judgment suffer the Soul to stay longer in the murthered Body,
that the cry of blood may make known the murtherer,
or may not so soon, for the same reason, call it totally
away."[68]

These specimens of Webster's temper of mind might
perhaps suffice to show with what slight justification he
has been regarded as a scientific rationalist. We must
not dismiss him, however, until we have scrutinized his
views on the subject of witchcraft itself. He passes for
a strong denier of the whole business of sorcery. We
shall find that this is a great mistake. So far from denying
the existence of witches, Webster is indignant at the
imputation that his theories and those of other like-minded
scholars should be interpreted in any such sense. ''If
I deny that a Witch cannot flye in the air, nor be transformed
or transubstantiated into a Cat, a Dog, or an Hare, or that
the Witch maketh any visible Covenant with the Devil,
or that he sucketh on their bodies, or that the Devil hath
carnal Copulation with them; I do not thereby deny either
the Being of Witches, nor other properties that they may
have, for which they may be so called: no more than if
I deny that a dog hath rugibility (which is only proper to
a Lion) doth it follow that I deny the being of a Dog, or
that he hath latrability?"[69] This sentence contains, in
effect, the sum and substance of Webster's negative
propositions on the subject.[70] Let us see what he holds
as affirmatives.

Though rejecting the theory of an external covenant
between the devil and a witch, Webster acknowledges
''an internal, mental, and spiritual League or Covenant
betwixt the Devil and all wicked persons.'' Further,
''this spiritual League in some respects and in some persons

---

[67] P. 308. On the astral spirit, see also pp. 312 ff.
[68] Page 310.
[69] Pages 10–11.
[70] See also pp. 267 ff.

may be, and is an explicit League, that is, the persons
that enter into it, are or may be conscious of it, and know
it to be so."[71]   Now there are certain persons, commonly
called witches, who are full of "hatred, malice, revenge
and envy," of which the devil is the "author and causer,"[72]
and these, by Satan's instigation, "do secretly and by
tradition learn strange poysons, philters and receipts
whereby they do much hurt and mischief.   Which most
strange wayes of poysoning, tormenting, and breeding
of unwonted things in the stomach and bellies of people,
have not been unknown unto many learned men and
Philosophers."[73]   Among · these effects of "an art more
than Diabolical," which has "been often practiced by
most horrible, malevolent, and wicked persons," is the
production of the plague.   There is no doubt of the fact.
There are "undeniable examples."   An unguent may be
prepared which is of such power that when it is smeared
upon the handles of doors, "those that do but lightly touch
them are forthwith infected."   In 1536 there was a conspiracy
of some forty persons in Italy, who caused the death of
many in this way.[74]   To such arts Webster ascribes the
dreadful outbreak of jail-fever at the Oxford assizes in
1579.   This was not, and could not be, the ordinary "prison
infection."   It was brought about by the contrivances
of one Roland Jenks, "a Popish recusant," who was
condemned for seditious words against the queen.   Jenks,
it seems, had procured strange poisons of a local apothecary,
and had made a kind of candle out of them.   As soon as
he was condemned, he lighted his candle, from which there
arose such a "damp," or steam, that the pestilence broke
out as we have seen.[75]   It is manifest, Webster holds,
"that these kind of people that are commonly called
Witches, are indeed (as both the Greek and Latin names
doe signifie) Poysoners, and in respect of their Hellish designs
are Diabolical, but the effects they procure flow from natural

---

[71] Page 73.
[72] Page 231.
[73] Pages 242-243.
[74] Page 244.
[75] Pages 245-246

Causes."[76]  This last proposition is, indeed, perhaps the chief point of Webster's book. Witches exist, and they do horrible things, but they accomplish their ends, not by the actual intervention of the devil and his imps, but by virtue of an acquaintance with little-known laws of nature. Another example, which cannot be quoted in detail, will make Webster's position perfectly clear. A man was afflicted with a dreadful disease. The cause was discovered to be the presence of an oaken pin in the corner of a courtyard. The pin was destroyed and the man drank birchen ale. He made a complete recovery. It is plain, according to Webster, that the pulling up and burning of the oaken pin "was with the help of the Birchen Ale the cure; but it can no wayes be judged necessary that the Devil should fix the Oak pin there, but that the Witch might do it himself. Neither can it be thought to be any power given by the Devil to the Oaken pin, that it had not by nature, for in all probability it will constantly by a natural power produce the same effect; only thus far the Devil had a hand in the action, to draw some wicked person to fix the pin there...., thereby to hurt and torture him."[77]

One is tempted to still further quotations from Webster's utterances on this topic, especially because his book has been much oftener mentioned than read. But we must rest content with one passage which sums up the whole matter:—'The opinions that we reject as foolish and impious are those we have often named before, to wit, that those that are vulgarly accounted Witches, make a visible and corporeal contract with the Devil, that he sucks upon their bodies, that he hath carnal copulation with them, that they are transubstantiated into Cats, Dogs, Squirrels, and the like, or that they raise tempests, and fly in the air. Other powers we grant unto them, to operate and effect whatsoever the force of natural imagination joyned with envy, malice and vehement desire of revenge, can perform or perpetrate, or whatsoever hurt may be done by secret poysons and such like wayes that work by meer natural means."[78]

---

[76] Page 247.
[77] Page 260.
[78] Page 267.

It is true that Webster opposed some of the current witch dogmas of his time. There are passages enough in his elaborate treatise which insist on the prevalence of fraud and melancholia. In his Epistle Dedicatory, which is addressed to five Yorkshire justices of the peace, he lays particular stress on the necessity of distinguishing between impostors and those unfortunate persons who are "under a mere passive delusion" that they are witches, and warns the magistrates not to believe impossible confessions. For all this he deserves honor.[79] Nor do I intend for a moment to suggest that the queer things (as we regard them now-a-days) which I have cited are in any manner discreditable to Webster. He was not exceptionally credulous, and he belonged to that advanced school of English physicians who, in the second half of the seventeenth century, upheld the general theories of Paracelsus and van Helmont in opposition to the outworn follies of the Galenists or regulars. He was a man of great erudition, of vast and varied experience, of uncommon mental gifts, and of passionate devotion to the truth. I admire him, but I must be pardoned if I am unable to see how he can be regarded as a tower of skeptical strength in the great witchcraft controversy. Even his admissions on the subject of the fallen angels are enough to destroy the efficiency of his denial of current notions about witchcraft. Once grant,

---

[79] Note, however, that the upholders of the current beliefs on witchcraft are also many times emphatic enough in similar cautionary remarks. A first-rate example is the following characteristic passage from Dr. Casaubon, whom Webster calls a "witchmonger":—

"And indeed, that the denying of *Witches*, to them that content themselves in the search of truth with a superficial view, is a very plausible cause; it cannot be denied. For if any thing in the world, (as we know all things in the world are) be liable to fraud, and imposture, and innocent mistake, through weakness and simplicity; this subject of Witches and Spirits is. . . How ordinary is it to mistake natural melancholy (not to speak of other diseases) for a Devil? And how much, too frequently, is both the disease increased, or made incurable; and the mistake confirmed, by many ignorant Ministers, who take every wild motion, or phansie, for a suggestion of the Devil? Whereas, in such a case, it should be the care of wise friends, to apply themselves to the Physician of the body, and not to entertain the other, (I speak it of *natural* melancholy) who probably may do more hurt, than good; but as the learned Naturalist doth allow, and advise? Excellent is the advice and counsel in this kind, of the Author of the book *de morbo Sacro* attributed to *Hippocrates*, which I could wish all men were bound to read, before they take upon them to visit sick folks, that are troubled with melancholy diseases" (A Treatise proving Spirits, etc., 1672, pp. 29–30: cf. p. 14, note 31, above).

as Webster does, that our atmosphere is peopled by legions upon legions of evil angels, delighting in sin, eager to work mischief, inimical to God and man, furnished with stores of acquired knowledge, and able to devise wicked thoughts and put them into our minds,[80] and it was idle to deny— in the face of the best philosophic and theological opinion of the ages—that these demonic beings can make actual covenants with witches or furnish them with the means of doing injury to their fellow-creatures.

" *A Witch*," according to Glanvill's definition, "*is one, who can do or seems to do strange things, beyond the known Power of Art and ordinary Nature, by vertue of a Confederacy with Evil Spirits*...The *strange things* are *really* performed, and are not all *Impostures* and *Delusions*. The Witch *occasions*, but is not the *Principal* Efficient, she seems to do it, but the *Spirit* performs the wonder, sometimes immediately, as in *Transportations* and *Possessions*, sometimes by applying other Natural Causes, as in raising *Storms*, and inflicting *Diseases*, sometimes using the *Witch* as an *Instrument*, and either by the Eyes or Touch, conveying Malign Influences: And these things are done by vertue of a *Covenant*, or *Compact* betwixt the *Witch* and an *Evil Spirit*. A *Spirit*, viz. an *Intelligent Creature* of the Invisible World, whether one of the Evil Angels called *Devils*, or an Inferiour *Dæmon* or *Spirit*, or a wicked *Soul* departed; but one that is able and ready for mischief, and whether altogether Incorporeal or not, appertains not to this Question."[81] Glanvill's book was well known to the Mathers. So was Webster's Displaying of Supposed Witchcraft.[82] Could there be a moment's doubt which of the two would appeal the more powerfully to their logical sense? Why, even we ourselves, if we look at the matter fairly,—taking into consideration Webster's whole case, and not merely such parts of it as accord with our preconceived opinions,—are forced to admit that Glanvill's position is much the stronger.

---

[80] Pages 219, 220, 224.
[81] Saducismus Triumphatus, Part II, ed. 1682, p. 4. (ed. 1726, pp. 225-226). Glanvill is here replying to Webster, whose book, it will be remembered, appeared in 1677.
[82] Increase Mather's copy is in the Harvard College Library.

In a well-known passage, in which the intellectual temper of Massachusetts before 1660 is contrasted with that of the next generation,[83] our classic New England essayist remarks that after 1660 the Colonists ''sank rapidly into provincials, narrow in thought, in culture, in creed.'' ''Such a pedantic portent as Cotton Mather,'' Lowell continues, ''would have been impossible in the first generation; he was the natural growth of the third.'' To discuss these epigrammatic theses would take us far beyond the limits of our present subject. One thing, however, must be said. Pedantry in the latter half of the seventeenth century was not confined to New England, nor to the ranks of those who were controversially styled the witchmongers. Meric Casaubon and Joseph Glanvill were not pedantic, but John Webster's Displaying of Supposed Witchcraft—which in some respects comes very near to being a great book—is a monument of pedantry, and John Webster was not a product of New England.

In Thomas Hobbes, whom we may next consider, we find a philosopher who was altogether incredulous on the subject of witchcraft. ''As for witches,'' he writes, ''I think not that their witchcraft is any real power; but yet that they are justly punished, for the false belief that they have that they can do such mischief, joined with their purpose to do it if they can; their trade being nearer to a new religion than to a craft or science.''[84] This dictum may accord with reason, but

---

[83] Lowell, New England Two Centuries Ago, Writings, Riverside edition, II, 73.

[84] Leviathan, i, 2 (English Works, ed. Molesworth, III, 9). Compare Hobbes's Dialogue between a Philosopher and a Student of the Common Law of England (English Works, VI, 96):—''L. I know not. Besides these crimes, there is conjuration, witchcraft, sorcery and enchantment; which are capital by the statute I James, c. 12.—P. But I desire not to discourse of that subject. For though without doubt there is some great wickedness signified by those crimes; yet I have ever found myself too dull to conceive the nature of them, or how the devil hath power to do so many things which witches have been accused of.'' Wier is far more humane, as well as more reasonable. If one holds, he writes, that witches are to be severely punished for their evil intent, let it be remembered that there is a great difference between sane and insane will. ''Quod si quis contentiose uoluntatem seuerius puniendam defendat, is primum distinguat inter uoluntatem hominis sani perfectam, quae in actum uere dirigi coeperit: et inter uitiatae mentis sensum, uel (si uoles) corruptam amentis uoluntatem: cui suo opere, quasi alterius esset, colludit diabolus, nec alius insulae uolentem subsequitur effectus.'' De Praestigiis Daemonum, vi, 21, ed. 1568, pp. 641-642.

one must admit that it was cold comfort for persons accused
of diabolical arts. And so was the more famous remark
of Selden: "The Law against Witches does not prove there
be any; but it punishes the Malice of those people, that
use such means, to take away mens lives. If one should
profess that by turning his Hat thrice, and crying Buz;
he could take away a man's life (though in truth he could
do no such thing) yet this were a just Law made by the
State, that whosoever should turn his Hat thrice, and cry
Buz; with an intention to take away a man's life, shall be put
to death."[85]   Bayle, shortly after the beginning of the
eighteenth century, agreed with Selden as to the justice
of putting "sorciers imaginaires" to death.[86]   Thomas
Ady, believing (like Scot, to whom he often refers) that
the witches and sorcerers of the Bible were mere cheats,
and that the same is true of all who pretend to similar
arts in modern times, is ready to admit the justice of the
death penalty in cases of fraud.   In describing the case
of a certain Master of Arts who was "condemned only for
using himself to the study and practice of the Jugling
craft," he concludes:—"If he had been a Jugler, or
practiser of that Craft to this end, to withstand the
Prophets when they wrought true miracles, as *Pha-
raohs* Juglers withstood *Moses*, or if he were one that
practised it to seduce the people after lying delusions,
to magnifie himself as a false Prophet, like *Simon
Magus* in the *Acts*, or to cause people to ascribe
miraculous power to him, or to seek to the Devil as our
common Deceivers, called good Witches, do, he was
deservedly condemned."[87]

Four dissenters from the current witchcraft dogma we
must pass over in silence—John Wagstaffe, Sir Robert
Filmer, Robert Calef, and Dr. Francis Hutchinson.  Calef
came too late to be really significant in our discussion;
Filmer's tract is a kind of *jeu d'esprit*, not likely to have

---

[85] Table-Talk, 1689, p. 59 (the first edition).  Selden died in 1654.
[86] Soldan, Geschichte der Hexenprozesse, ed. Heppe, II, 243.
[87] A Candle in the Dark: or, A Treatise concerning the Nature of Witches & Witchcraft, 1656, p. 41.

had any influence except upon lawyers;[88] and Wagstaffe's book is a quite inconsiderable affair. Yet, in parting, we must not neglect an odd remark concerning two out of the four—as well as one other, John Webster, whose lucubrations we have already criticised—a remark which, occurring as it does in a work of much learning and unusual distinction, illustrates in striking fashion the inaccuracy which we have already had occasion to notice, now and again, in recent writers who have busied themselves with the abstruse and complicated subject of witchcraft. President White, in his Warfare of Science with Theology, expresses his admiration for Webster, Wagstaffe, and Hutchinson in the following terms:—'But especially should honour be paid to the younger men in the Church, who wrote at length against the whole system: such men as Wagstaffe and Webster and Hutchinson, who in the humbler ranks of the clergy stood manfully for truth, with the certainty that by so doing they were making their own promotion impossible.'[89] Of the three men whom Dr. White thus commends for renouncing all hope of ecclesiastical preferment, the first, John Webster, was sixty-seven years old when he published his book; he had long been a Non-Conformist, and he describes himself on his title-page as "Practitioner in Physick." The second, John Wagstaffe, was a gentleman of independent means who damaged his health by "continual bibbing of strong and high tasted liquors"[90] and who was not in orders at all; the third, Dr. Francis Hutchinson, was Chaplain in Ordinary to King George I. when he published his Essay and was advanced to a bishopric two years after the first edition of the book appeared."[91]

---

[88] Sir Robert Filmer's brief tract, An Advertisement to the Jury-men of England, touching Witches, was occasioned, according to the Preface, by "the late Execution of Witches at the Summer Assises in Kent." It was first published in 1652, and may be found annexed to the Free-holders Grand Inquest, 1679. The case which elicited Sir Robert's little book is reported in A Prodigious & Tragicall History of the Arraignment, Tryall, Confession, and Condemnation of six Witches at Maidstone, in Kent, at the Assises there held in July, Fryday 30, this present year, 1652 (London, 1652, reprinted 1837).

[89] A. D. White, A History of the Warfare of Science with Theology, 1896, I, 362.

[90] Wood, Athenæ Oxonienses, ed. Bliss, III, 1114.

[91] Dr. Hutchinson's admirable work, An Historical Essay concerning Witchcraft, which still remains one of the most valuable treatises on this subject that we have,

When in 1692 and 1693, we come to The Enchanted
World (De Betoverde Weereld)[92] of the Dutch preacher
and theologian Balthasar Bekker, we arrive at a method
of opposing the witch dogma different from anything we
have so far examined. Bekker was fully aware of the
difficulties of his theme, and he had an uncommonly logical
head. His method is perfect. He first sets forth the spiritual
beliefs of the Greeks and Romans and their practices in
the way of sorcery. Then he shows—with an anticipation
of the process so often used by the modern anthropological
school—that the same doctrines and practices are found
among "the pagans of the present day,"—in Northern
Europe, in Asia, in Africa, and in America, as well as among
the ancient Jews. The Manichæan heresy, he contends,
was a mélange of pagan and Jewish doctrines. These
doctrines—heathen, Jewish, and Manichæan—early became
current among Christians. Hence, Christians in general
now hold that all sorts of extraordinary happenings are
due to the activity of the devil. Thus Bekker succeeds
in explaining the primary conceptions of modern demonology
and witchcraft as derived from heathen sources.[93]

Bekker's next task is to define body and spirit, according
to reason and the Bible. Both body and spirit are creatures.
God, being perfect and increate, is neither body nor spirit,
but superior to both. He is called a spirit in the Bible,
simply because there is no better word to express the divine
nature, but that nature is different from what is ordinarily
meant by the term. God being the governor of the world,
we have no ground for believing that there are demigods
(dæmons in the Greek sense) or vice-gods. Apart from the
Scriptures, reason affords us no proof that there are any spirits
except men's souls. The Scriptures, however, teach that
there are good angels, of whom Michael is the chief, and

---

was published in 1718. It appeared in a second edition in 1720, in which year he
was appointed Bishop of Down and Connor.

[92] I have used a copy of the French translation,—Le Monde Enchanté, Amsterdam,
1694. This was made by Bekker's direction and revised by him. Each of the four
volumes has a separate dedication, and each dedication (in the Harvard College
copy) is authenticated by Bekker's autograph signature.

[93] This concludes Bekker's First Book.

bad angels, whose prince is the devil. Beyond this, we learn practically nothing from the Bible with regard to a hierarchy of angels or of devils. Demoniacal possession was a natural disease: it had nothing to do with evil spirits. Such devils as are mentioned in Scripture are not said to be vassals of Satan; in many cases we are to understand the word "devil" merely as a figure of speech for a wicked man. There is no warrant in Holy Writ for the belief that Satan can appear to mortals under different forms, nor for the powers vulgarly ascribed to him and his supposed demonic household. In particular, there is no scriptural warrant for the opinion that Satan or his imps can injure men bodily or even suggest evil thoughts to them. The devil and the evil angels are damned in hell; they have not the power to move about in this world. The only way in which Satan is responsible for the sins which we commit is through his having brought about the fall of Adam, so that men are now depraved creatures, prone to sin. There is no place in the divine government for particular suggestions to wickedness, made from time to time, since the Fall, either by Satan himself or by any of his train. Diabolical influence upon mankind was confined to the initial temptation in Eden. Since Adam, neither Satan nor any evil spirit has been active in this world in any manner whatever, spiritual or corporeal. God rules, and the devil is not a power to be reckoned with at all. These revolutionary propositions Bekker proves, to his own satisfaction, not only from reason, but from the Word of God.[94]

Here at last we have a rational method. Bekker is not content with half-measures; he lays the axe to the root. There is a devil, to be sure, and there are fallen angels; but neither the one nor the other can have anything to do with the life and actions of mortal men. Practically, then, the devil is non-existent. We may disregard him entirely. If Bekker's propositions are admitted, the stately fabric of demonology and witchcraft crumbles in an instant. And nothing less drastic than such propositions will suffice

---

[94] What precedes is, in substance, Bekker's Book II.

to make witchcraft illogical or incredible. Bekker's
argument, we see at once, is utterly different from anything
that his predecessors had attempted.

It now becomes necessary for Bekker to proceed to discuss
those passages in the Bible which appear to justify the
common beliefs in sorcery and witchcraft. These beliefs
are contrary to reason, but, if they rest upon revelation,
they must still be accepted, for Bekker regards himself
as an orthodox Christian of the Dutch Reformed Church.
Accordingly Bekker takes up every scriptural passage
which mentions witches, enchanters, diviners, and the like,
and interprets them all in such a way that they lend no
support to current beliefs in the reality of compacts with
the devil, of magic, or of witchcraft. Whatever magicians
and witches, so-called, may think of their own performances,
there is nothing in Scripture, as interpreted by this bold
and expert theologian and unsurpassed dialectician, to
warrant us in believing in intercourse with Satan, or in
his intervention, with or without the mediation of sorcerers
and witches, in human life as it is to-day.[95]

But, Bekker hastens to admit, there remains a huge mass
of recent testimony which is regarded by almost everybody
as sufficient to establish the existence of sorcery and witchcraft, whether such things are recognized in the Bible or
not. To this testimony Bekker devotes the Fourth (and
last) Book of his treatise.

He first points out that all such testimony is prejudiced,
since it comes from persons who have a fixed and, so to
speak, an inherited belief in the truth of the marvels whose
very existence is in question. He then examines a great
body of material, with splendid sobriety and common sense.
This is perhaps the most interesting part of his work to
us,—though in fact it is less original than much of what
precedes, since all opponents of the witch dogma, beginning
with Wier, had attacked the evidence in many particulars,
and since even those scholars and theologians who supported
the dogma most effectively—like Glanvill—had granted

---

[95] This is the substance of Bekker's Third Book.

without hesitation that fraud and delusion played a large
part in the accumulation of testimony. Bekker's treatment of the subject, however, is better than anything of
the kind that had been written before. Fraud, terror,
hysteria, insanity, illusion of the senses,—due to disease
or to what we should now call hypnotic or semi-hypnotic
conditions,—unknown laws of nature—these are the sources
from which he derives his interpretation of the evidence.
This part of his work, then, has a singularly modern tone,
and gives the author a valid claim to rank as an enlightened
psychologist.

It has seemed advisable to give particular attention
to Bekker's Enchanted World because of its singular
merits, as well as on account of the distinguished position
which it deservedly holds among the books which oppose
the belief in witchcraft. In strictness, however, we are not
bound to include this work in our survey of seventeenth-
century opinion, since it did not appear in season to exert
any influence on New England at the time of the Salem
prosecution. The first two Books of Bekker's work were
published in 1691; the second two, which deal specifically
with witchcraft, in 1693. The trouble in Salem began in
February, 1692, and the prosecution collapsed in January,
1693. It is certain that New England scholars knew nothing
about the first two Books when they were engaged in witch
trials, and the last two were not published until the trials
had come to an end. But this matter of dates need not
be insisted on. Even if our ancestors had received advance
sheets of The Enchanted World, their opinions would not,
in all probability, have been in the slightest degree affected.
Indeed, the reception which Bekker's treatise met with
in his own country is a plain indication of the temper of
the times in this business of witchcraft. The publication
of the first two Books in 1691 was the signal for a storm
of denunciation. The Dutch press teemed with replies
and attacks. Bekker was instantly called to account by
the authorities of the Reformed Church. Complicated
ecclesiastical litigation ensued, with the result that the
Synod of North Holland issued a decree declaring Bekker

"intolerable as teacher in the Reformed Church" and expelling him from his ministerial office (August 7, 1692).[96] Soon after, the Church Council of Amsterdam voted to exclude him from the Lord's Supper (August 17),[97] and he was never admitted to communion again. He died on June 11, 1698.[98]

Another reason for going so fully into Bekker's arguments is that they give us an excellent chance to take up a question which is of cardinal importance in weighing the whole matter of witchcraft. I refer, of course, to the question of Biblical exegesis.

If we wish to treat our forefathers fairly, we are required to criticise the few opponents of the witch dogma in a really impartial way. We ought not to commend such portions of their argument as chance to square with our own ideas, and ignore the rest. We must review their case as a whole, so as to discover how far it was right or reasonable on the basis of their own postulates. We must test the correctness of their premises, as well as the accuracy of their logic.

This process we have gone through with already in several instances. We have seen that all the opponents of witchcraft so far examined struggle to maintain a position that is strategically indefensible, either because they admit too much, or because they ignore certain difficulties, or

---

[96] "De Christelijke Synodus . . . heeft, . . . met eenparigheyd van stemmen, den selven Dr. Bekker verklaart intolerabel als Leeraar in de Gereformeerde Kerke; en vervolgens hem van sijn Predik-dienst geremoveert" (decree in W. P. C. Knuttel, Balthasar Bekker de Bestrijder van het Bijgeloof, the Hague, 1906, p. 315).

[97] Knuttel, p. 319.

[98] Knuttel, p. 357. Strictly speaking, it was not for his denial of modern witchcraft that Bekker was punished, for it is in the last two books of his treatise that he deals particularly with this subject, and these did not appear until after he had been unfrocked. Still, his Second Book, which got him into trouble, contains all the essentials. It denies the power of the devil and wicked spirits to afflict men, and holds that the demoniacs of the New Testament were neither possessed nor obsessed, but merely sufferers from disease. For a full analysis of Bekker's work and an account of the opposition which it roused, see Knuttel, chap. v, pp. 188 ff.; for the ecclesiastical proceedings against Bekker, see chap. vi, pp. 270 ff. The various editions and translations of De Betoverde Weereld are enumerated by van der Linde in his Balthasar Bekker, Bibliographie (the Hague, 1869), where may also be found a long list of the books and pamphlets which the work called forth. There is a good account of Bekker's argument in Soldan's Geschichte der Hexenprosesse, neu bearbeitet von Dr. Heinrich Heppe (Stuttgart, 1880), II, 233 ff. See also Roskoff, Geschichte des Teufels, Leipzig, 1869, II, 445 ff.

because they are frankly eccentric. It does not help their
case to contend that what they admit or what they ignore
does not signify from our present scientific point of view.
It *did* signify *then*. The only man whose argument covers
the ground completely and affords a thorough and consistent
theory on which a seventeenth-century Christian was
logically justified in rejecting witchcraft and demoniacal
possession as facts of everyday experience is Balthasar
Bekker.

Now the truth or falsity of Bekker's very radical conclu-
sions hinged—for Bekker himself and for his contemporaries
—on the soundness of his Biblical exegesis. If his way of
disposing of those passages which mention devils and
witches and diviners and familiar spirits is not justifiable—
if the Biblical writers did not mean what he thinks they
meant—then his whole case goes to pieces. In discussing
the witchcraft dogma of the seventeenth century, we must
accept the Bible, for the nonce, as the men of the seventeenth
century (Bekker included) accepted it—as absolutely true
in every detail, as dynamically inspired by the Holy Ghost,
as a complete rule of faith and practice. Modern views
on this subject have no *locus standi*.

Now, if we only keep these fundamental principles firmly
in mind, we shall have no doubt as to the outcome. Beyond
question, the Bible affords ample authority for belief in
demoniacal possession, in necromancy, in the ability of
Satan and his cohorts to cause physical phenomena,
and in the power of sorcerers to work miracles.[99] True,
not all the details of the witchcraft dogma rest upon Biblical

---

[99] Theologians took infinite pains to distinguish between miracles (*miracula*),
which could be wrought by divine power only, and the kind of wonders (*mira*)
which Satan worked. See, for example, William Perkins, A Discourse of the Damned
Art of Witchcraft, 1608, pp. 12 ff., 18 ff.; Del Rio, Disquisitiones Magicæ, lib. ii,
quæstio 7, ed. 1616, pp. 103 ff. Sir Robert Filmer, in An Advertisement to the Jury-
men of England, Touching Witches (appended to The Free-holders Grand Inquest,
1679; cf. p. 34, note 88, above), makes merry with such fine-spun distinctions. "Both
[Perkins and Del Rio]," he says, "seem to agree in this, that he had need be an
admirable or profound Philosopher, that can distinguish between a Wonder and a
Miracle; it would pose *Aristotle* himself, to tell us every thing that can be done by
the power of Nature, and what things cannot; for there be daily many things found
out, and daily more may be, which our Fore-fathers never knew to be possible in
Nature" (pp. 322-323). Cf. Calef, More Wonders of the Invisible World, 1700, p. 35.

authority, but enough of them do so rest to make the case of those who uphold the traditional opinion substantially unassailable, except upon the purely arbitrary assumption that all these wonders, though formerly actual, have ceased in recent times.[100] Bekker's exegesis is erroneous in countless particulars and presents an altogether mistaken view of Biblical doctrines. As interpreters of the language of Scripture, the orthodox theologians of his time, who pinned their faith to witchcraft, were nearer right than he was. And what is true of Bekker's exegesis, is equally true of that followed by all previous opponents of the witchcraft dogma. My reason for not referring to this point in criticising their books is obvious. Bekker has gone farther, and succeeded better, in explaining away the testimony of Scripture than any of the others. It is more than fair to them to rest this part of the case upon his success or failure. If Bekker falls, all of them certainly fall,—and Bekker falls.[101]

From our cursory examination of the works put forth by some of the chief opponents of the witch dogma, it must be evident that none of these works can have had a very profound influence on the beliefs of the seventeenth century,-their function was rather, by keeping discussion alive, to prepare for the change of sentiment which took place soon after 1700, in what we are accustomed to call "the age of prose and reason." Such an examination as we have given to these books was necessary to establish the proposition with which we set out,—that our ancestors in 1692 were

---

[100] Cf. Soldan, Geschichte der Hexenprosesse, ed. Heppe, II, 243:—"Zu derjenigen freieren Kritik der biblischen Schriften selbst sich zu erheben, welche das Vorhandensein gewisser, aus den Begriffen der Zeit geschöpfter dämonologischen Vorstellungen in der Bibel anerkennt, ohne daraus eine bindende Norm für den Glauben herzuleiten, —diess war freilich erst einem späteren Zeitalter vorbehalten. Bekker kannte, um seine sich ihm aufdringende philosophische Ueberzeugung mit der Bibel zu versöhnen, keinen andern Weg, als den der üblichen Exegese, und daher kommt es, dass diese nicht überall eine ungezwungene ist." It is instructive to note the pains which Sir Walter Scott takes, in his Second Letter on Demonology and Witchcraft, to harmonise the Bible with his views on these subjects.

[101] To avoid all possibility of misapprehension I shall venture to express my own feelings. The two men who appeal to me most in the whole affair of witchcraft are Friedrich Spee, the Jesuit, and Balthasar Bekker, the "intolerable" pastor of Amsterdam. But what I feel, and what all of us feel, is not to the purpose. There has been too much feeling in modern discussions of witchcraft already.

42

in accord with the practically universal belief of their day. It has shown more than this, however,—it has demonstrated that their position was logically and scripturally stronger than that of their antagonists, provided we judge the matter (as we are in honor bound to do) on the basis of those doctrines as to supernaturalism and the inspiration of the Bible that were alike admitted by both sides. We may repeat, then, with renewed confidence, the statement already made:—Our forefathers believed in witchcraft, not because they were Puritans, not because they were Colonials, not because they were New Englanders, but because they were men of their own time and not of ours.

Another point requires consideration if we would arrive at a just judgment on the Salem upheaval. It is frequently stated, and still oftener assumed, that the outbreak at Salem was peculiar in its virulence, or, at all events, in its intensity. This is a serious error, due, like other misapprehensions, to a neglect of the history of witchcraft as a whole. The fact is, the Salem excitement was the opposite of peculiar,—it was perfectly typical. The European belief in witchcraft, which our forefathers shared without exaggerating it, was a constant quantity. It was always present, and continuously fraught with direful possibilities. But it did not find expression in a steady and regular succession of witch trials. On the contrary, it manifested itself at irregular intervals in spasmodic outbursts of prosecution. Notable examples occurred at Geneva from 1542 to 1546;[102] at Wiesensteig, Bavaria, in 1562 and 1563;[103] in the Electorate of Trier from 1587 to 1593;[104] among the Basques of Labourd in 1609;[105] at Mohra in Sweden in 1669 and 1670.[106]

---

[102] Sigmund Riezler, Geschichte der Hexenprozesse in Bayern, Stuttgart, 1896, p. 143.

[103] Ibid.

[104] Soldan, Geschichte der Hexenprozesse, revised by Heppe, II, 37; cf. G. L. Burr, The Fate of Dietrich Flade, 1891 (reprinted from the Papers of the American Historical Association, V).

[105] Jean d'Espaignet and Pierre de Lancre, the special commissioners, are said to have condemned more than 600 in four months (Soldan, ed. Heppe, II, 162; cf. Baissac, Les Grands Jours de la Sorcellerie, 1890, p. 401). I have no certain evidence of the accuracy of these figures, for I have seen only one of de Lancre's two books, and I find in it no distinct statement of the number of witches convicted. He makes various remarks, however, which seem to show that 600 is no exaggeration. Thus he

In the district of Ortenau, in Baden, witchcraft prosecutions suddenly broke out, after a considerable interval, in 1627, and there were seventy-three executions in three years.[107] From the annals of witchcraft in Great Britain one may cite the following cases:—1581, at St. Osith's, in Essex;[108] 1590-1597, in Scotland;[109] 1612, at Lancaster,[110] and again in 1633;[111] 1616, in Leicestershire;[112] 1645-1647, the Hop-

says that the Parliament of Bordeaux, under whose authority he acted, condemned "an infinity" of sorcerers to death in 1609 (Tableau de l'Inconstance des Mauvais Anges et Demons, Paris, 1613, p. 100). "On fait estat qu'il y a trente mille ames en ce pays de Labourt, contant ceux qui sont en voyage sur mer, & que parmy tout ce peuple, il y a bien peu de familles qui ne touchent au Sortilege par quelque bout" (p. 38). The commission lasted from July to November (pp. 66, 456, 470); besides those that the two commissioners tried during this period, they left behind them so many witches and wizards that the prisons of Bordeaux were crowded and it became necessary to lodge the defendants in the ruined château du Hâ (pp. 144, 560). Cf. pp. 35 ff., 64, 92, 114, 546. The panic fear that witchcraft excites is described by de Lancre in a striking passage:—"Qu'il n'y ayt qu'vne seule sorciere dans vn grand village, dans peu de temps vous voyes tant d'enfans perdus, tant de femmes enceintes perdas leur fruit, tant de haut mal donné à des pauures creatures, tant d'animaux perdus, tant de fruicts gastes, que le foudre ni autre fleau du ciel ne sont rien en comparaison" (pp. 543-544).

[106] An Account of what Happened in the Kingdom of Sweden, in the Years 1669, 1670 and Upwards, translated from the German by Anthony Horneck, and included in Glanvill's Saducismus Triumphatus, ed. 1682 (ed. 1726, pp. 474 ff.). Horneck's version is from a tract entitled, Translation . . . Der Königl. Herren Comissarien gehaltenes Protocol uber die entdeckte Zauberey in dem Dorff Mohra und umbliegenden Orten, the Hague, 1670. Cf. Thomas Wright, Narratives of Sorcery and Magic, II, 244 ff.; Soldan, ed. Heppe, II, 175 ff.; Vilhelm Bang, Hexevæsen og Hexeforfølgelser især i Danmark, Copenhagen, 1896, pp. 48 ff. This is what Mr. Upham calls Cotton Mather's "favorite Swedish case" (Salem Witchcraft and Cotton Mather, Morrisania, 1869, p. 20). It was, in a manner, "Leonato's Hero, your Hero, every man's Hero" toward the end of the seventeenth century, since it was one of the most recent instances of witchcraft on a large scale. The good angel in white who is one of the features of the Mohra case appears much earlier in England: see Potts, Wonderfull Discoverie of Witches, 1613, Chetham Society reprint, sig. L (a reference which may serve as a note to Mr. Upham's essay, just cited, p. 34).

[107] Frans Volk, Hexen in der Landvogtei Ortenau und Reichsstadt Offenburg, Lahr, 1882, pp. 24-25, 58 ff.

[108] Scot, Discoverie of Witchcraft, 1584, p. 543; F. Hutchinson, Historical Essay, 2d ed., p. 38; W. W., A True and Just Recorde, of the Information [etc.] of all the Witches, taken at S. Oses (London, 1582). For extracts from W. W.'s book I am indebted to Mr. Wallace Notestein, of Yale University.

[109] F. Legge, The Scottish Review, XVIII, 261 ff.

[110] Thomas Potts, The Wonderfull Discoverie of Witches in the Countie of Lancaster (London, 1613), reprinted by the Chetham Society, 1845; Thomas Wright, Narratives of Sorcery and Magic, Chap. xxiii.

[111] Whalley Lancashire, . by Whitaker, pp. 213 ff.; Chetham Society reprint of Potts, as above, pp. lix ff.; Wright, as above, Chap. xxiii; Heywood and Brome's play, The Late Lancashire Witches, 1634; Calendar of State Papers, Domestic Series, 1634-1635, pp. 77-79, 98, 129-130, 141, 152; Historical Manuscripts Commission, 10th Report, Appendix, Part IV, p. 433; 12th Report, Appendix, Part II, p. 53, cf. p. 77; Notes and Queries, 3d Series, V, 259, 385.

[112] Nichols, History and Antiquities of the County of Leicester, II, 471.*

kins prosecution;[113] 1649-1650, at Newcastle-on-Tyne;[114] 1652, at Maidstone, in Kent;[115] 1682, at Exeter.[116] The sudden outbreak of witch trials in the Bermudas in 1651 is also worthy of attention.[117]

It is unnecessary for us to consider how much of the evidence offered at witch trials in England was actually true. Some of the defendants were pretty bad characters, and it would be folly to maintain that none of them tried to cause the sickness or death of their enemies by maltreating clay images or by other arts which they supposed would avail. Besides, now and then an injury is testified to which may well have been inflicted without diabolical aid. Thus Ann Foster, who was hanged for witchcraft at Northampton in 1674, confessed that she had set a certain grazier's barns on fire, and there is much reason to believe her, for she was under considerable provocation.[118] As to occult or super-normal powers and practices, we may leave their discussion to the psychologists. With regard to this aspect of the Salem troubles, we must accept, as substantially in accordance with the facts, the words of Dr. Poole: "No man of any reputation who lived in that generation, and saw what transpired at Salem Village and its vicinity, doubted that there was some influence then exerted which could not be explained by the known laws of matter or of mind."[119] Even Thomas Brattle, in speaking of the confessing witches, many of whom he says he has "again and again seen and heard," cannot avoid the hypothesis of demoniacal action. They are, he feels certain, "deluded, imposed upon, and

---

[113] See pp. 7 and 58.

[114] Whitelocke's Memorials, Dec. 13, 1649, ed. 1732, p. 434; Brand, Popular Antiquities, ed. Hazlitt, III, 80; Ralph Gardner, England's Grievance Discovered, in Relation to the Coal-Trade, 1655 (reprinted, North Shields, 1849, Chap. 53, pp. 168 ff.).

[115] A Prodigious & Tragicall History of the Arraignment [etc.] of Six Witches at Maidstone . . . Digested by H. F. Gent, 1652 (reprinted in an Account, etc., London, 1837).

[116] A True and Impartial Relation of the Informations against Three Witches, 1682.

[117] Sir J. H. Lefroy, Memorials of the Discovery and Early Settlement of the Bermudas or Somers Islands, II, 601 ff.

[118] A Full and True Relation of the Tryal [etc.] of Ann Foster, London, 1674 (Northampton, reprinted by Taylor & Son, 1878). Cf. W. Ruland, Steirische Hexenprosesse, in Steinhausen's Zeitschrift für Kulturgeschichte, 2. Ergänsungsheft, Weimar, 1898, pp. 45 ff.

[119] N. E. Hist. Gen. Register, XXIV, 382.

under the influence of some evil spirit; and therefore unfit to be evidences either against themselves, or any one else. "[120]

One common misapprehension to which the historians of witchcraft are liable comes from their failure to perceive that the immediate responsibility for actual prosecution rests frequently, if not in the majority of instances, on the rank and file of the community or neighborhood. This remark is not made in exculpation of prosecutors and judges, —for my purpose in this discussion is not to extenuate anybody's offences or to shift the blame from one man's shoulders to another. What is intended is simply to remind the reader of a patent and well-attested fact which is too often overlooked in the natural tendency of historians to find some notable personage to whom their propositions, commendatory or damaging, may be attached. A prosecution for witchcraft presupposes a general belief among the common people in the reality of the crime. But this is not all. It presupposes likewise the existence of a body of testimony, consisting of the talk of the neighborhood, usually extending back over a considerable stretch of years, with regard to certain persons who have the reputation of being witches, cunning men, and so on. It also presupposes the belief of the neighborhood that various strange occurrences,—such as storms, bad crops, plagues of grasshoppers and caterpillars, loss of pigs or cattle, cases of lunacy or hysteria or chorea or wasting sickness,—are due to the malice of those particular suspects and their unknown confederates. These strange occurrences, be it remembered, are not the fictions of a superstitious or distempered imagination, they are—most of them—things that have really taken place; they are the *res gestae* of the prosecution, without which it could never have come about, or, having begun, could never have continued. And further, in very many instances of prosecution for witchcraft, there have been among the accused, persons

---

[120] Letter of Oct. 8, 1692, Mass. Hist. Soc. Collections, V, 65. Compare, on the whole question, the remarks of Professor Wendell in his interesting paper, Were the Salem Witches Guiltless? (Historical Collections of the Essex Institute, XXIX, republished in his Stelligeri and Other Essays concerning America, New York, 1893) and in his Cotton Mather, pp. 93 ff.

who believed themselves to be witches,—or who had, at any rate, pretended to extraordinary powers and—in many instances—had either used their uncanny reputation to scare their enemies or to get money by treating diseases of men and cattle. And finally, the habit of railing and brawling, of uttering idle but malignant threats, and, on the other hand, the habit of applying vile epithets—including that of ''witch,''—to one's neighbors in the heat of anger— customs far more prevalent in former times than now— also resulted in the accumulation of a mass of latent or potential testimony which lay stored up in people's memories ready to become kinetic whenever the machinery of the law should once begin to move.[121]

Nobody will ask for evidence that railing and brawling went on in colonial New England, that our forefathers sometimes called each other bad names, or that slander was a common offence.[122] That suspicion of witchcraft was rife in various neighborhoods years before the Salem outbreak, is proved, not only by the records of sporadic cases that came before the courts,[123] but by some of the evidence in the Salem prosecution itself.

That the initial responsibility for prosecution usually rested with the neighborhood or community might further be shown by many specific pieces of testimony. The terrible prosecution in Trier toward the close of the sixteenth century is a case in point. ''Since it was commonly

---

[121] A long and curious list of cases of defamation may be seen in a volume of Depositions and other Ecclesiastical Proceedings from the County of Durham, extending from 1311 to the Reign of Elisabeth, edited by James Raine for the Surtees Society in 1845 (Publications, XXI). Thus, in 1566-67, Margaret Lambert accuses John Lawson of saying ''that she was a chermer'' (p. 84); about 1569 Margaret Reed is charged with calling Margaret Howhett ''a horse goodmother water wych'' (p. 91); in 1572, Thomas Fewler deposed that he ''hard Elisabeth Anderson caull . . . Anne Burden 'crowket handyd wytch.' He saith the words was spoken audiently there; ther might many have herd them, beinge spoken so neigh the crose and in the towne gait as they were'' (p. 247). So in 1691 Alice Bovill complained of a man who had said to her, ''Thou bewitched my stot'' (North Riding Record Society, Publications, IX, 6). See also Historical Manuscripts Commission, Report on Manuscripts in Various Collections, I, 283; Lefroy, Bermudas or Somers Islands, II, 629 (no. 15).

[122] See, for example, Mr. Noble's edition of the Records of the Court of Assistants, II, 43, 72, 85, 94, 95, 104, 131, 136,—all between 1633 and 1644.

[123] See Drake's Annals of Witchcraft in New England; Noble's Records, as above, I, 11, 31, 33, 159, 188, 228, 229, 233.

believed," writes Linden, an eyewitness, "that the continued failure of the crops for many years was caused by witches
and wizards through diabolical malice, the whole country
rose up for the annihilation of the witches."[124]   To like
purpose are the words of the admirable Jesuit, Friedrich
Spee, in the closing chapter of the most powerful and convincing protest against witch trials ever written—that chapter
which the author begged every magistrate in Germany
to mark and weigh, whether he read the rest of the book
or not:—"Incredible are the superstition, the envy, the
slanders and backbitings, the whisperings and gossip of
the common people in Germany, which are neither punished
by magistrates nor reproved by preachers.  These are
the causes that first rouse suspicion of witchcraft.  All
the punishments of divine justice with which God has
threatened men in the Holy Scriptures are held to come from
witches.  God and nature no longer do anything,—witches,
everything.  Hence it is that all demand, with violent out-
cry, that the magistracy shall proceed against the witches,
whom only their own tongues have made so numerous."[125]

As for England, the annals of witchcraft are full of instances
which show where the initial responsibility rests in particular
prosecutions.  Two examples will serve as well as many.

Roger North, the distinguished lawyer, who was at Exeter
in 1682, when a famous witch trial occurred,[126] gives a

---

[124] "Quia vulgo creditum, multorum annorum continuatam sterilitatem à strigibus
et maleficis diabolicâ invidiâ causari; tota patria in extinctionem maleficarum insur-
rexit" (as quoted from the autograph MS. in the Trier Stadt-Bibliothek by G. L.
Burr, The Fate of Dietrich Flade, p. 51, Papers of the American Historical Association, V).

[125] "Incredibile vulgi apud Germanos, & maxime (quod pudet dicere) Catholicos
superstitio, invidia, calumniæ, detractationes, susurrationes & similia, quæ nec Magistratus punit, nec concionatores arguunt, suspicionem magiæ primum excitant.
Omnes divinæ punitiones, quas in sacris literis Deus minatus est, à Sagis sunt.  Nihil
jam amplius Deus facit aut natura, sed Sagæ omnia.   2. Unde impetu omnes
clamant ut igitur inquirat Magistratus in Sagas, quas non nisi ipsi suis linguis tot
fecerunt" (Cautio Criminalis, seu de Processibus contra Sagas Liber, 2d ed., 1695, pp.
387-388; cf. Dubium xv, pp. 67-68, Dubium xxxiv, pp. 231-232).  Spee's book came
out anonymously in 1631, and, unlike most works on this side of the question, had
immediate results.  Spee had no doubt of the existence of witchcraft (Dubium i, pp.
1 ff., Dubium iii, pp. 7-8); his experience, however, had taught him that most of
those condemned were innocent.

[126] The case is reported in A True and Impartial Relation of the Informations
against Three Witches [etc.], 1682, which is reprinted in Howell's State Trials, VIII,
1017 ff.

vivid account of the popular excitement:—[127] "The women were very old, decrepit, and impotent, and were brought to the assizes with as much noise and fury of the rabble against them as could be shewed on any occasion. The stories of their acts were in everyone's mouth, and they were not content to belie them in the country, but even in the city where they were to be tried miracles were fathered upon them, as that the judges' coach was fixed upon the castle bridge, and the like. All which the country believed, and accordingly persecuted the wretched old creatures. A less zeal in a city or kingdom hath been the overture of defection and revolution, and if these women had been acquitted, it was thought that the country people would have committed some disorder."[128]

Our second example is a very notable case, which occurred in 1712,—that of Jane Wenham, the last witch condemned to death in England. Jane Wenham had a dispute with a neighboring farmer, who called her a witch. She complained to the local magistrate, Sir Henry Chauncy. He referred the dispute to the parson of the parish, who, after hearing both sides, admonished the wranglers to live at peace and sentenced the farmer to pay Jane a shilling. The old crone was not pleased. Shortly after, one of the clergyman's servants, a young woman, was strangely afflicted. Jane was brought to trial. Every effort seems to have been made by the court to put a stop to the affair, but the local feeling was so strong, and the witnesses and complainants were so many (including the clergymen of two parishes) that nothing could be done. The official

---

[127] Autobiography, chap. x, ed. Jessopp, 1887, pp. 131-132. North gives a similar account of the same trial, with some general observations of great interest, in his Life of the Lord Keeper Guilford, I, 267-269 (ed. 1826). It is not clear whether North was present at the trial or not. It is important to notice that North wrote his biographies late in life and that his death did not take place until 1736, the year in which the statute against witchcraft was repealed.

[128] North remarks that Guilford (then Francis North, Chief Justice of the Common Pleas) "had really a concern upon him at what happened; which was, that his brother Raymond's passive behavior should let those poor women die" (Life of the Lord Keeper Guilford, I, 267). Raymond was, to be sure, the judge who presided at the trial, but Francis North cannot be allowed to have all the credit which his brother Roger would give him, for he refused to reprieve the convicted witches (see his letter, quoted at p. 34, above).

who drew up the indictment endeavored to make the whole affair ridiculous by refusing to use any other phraseology in describing the alleged crime than "conversing with the devil in the form of a cat." But the well-meant device only intensified the feeling against the witch. Mr. Justice Powell, who presided, did what he could to induce the jury to acquit, but in vain. They brought in a verdict of guilty, and he was obliged to pass sentence of death. He suspended the execution of the sentence, however, and secured the royal pardon,—to the intense indignation of the neighborhood. Here we have a jury of the vicinage, accurately reflecting the local sentiment, and insisting on carrying out its belief in witchcraft to the bitter end, despite all that the judge could do.[129]   It is well to note that the clergymen involved in the prosecution were not New England Puritans, and that the whole affair took place just ten years after the last execution of a witch in Massachusetts. Of itself, this incident might suffice to silence those who ascribe the Salem outbreak to the influence of certain distinguished men, as well as those who maintain that the New Englanders were more superstitious than their fellow-citizens at home, that their Puritanism was somehow to blame for it, and that witchcraft was practically dead in the Mother Country when the Salem outbreak took place.[130]

---

[129] The following pamphlets (all in the Harvard College Library) appeared in London in 1712: (1) A Full and Impartial Account of the Discovery of Sorcery and Witchcraft, practis'd by Jane Wenham of Walkerne in Hertfordshire; (2) The Case of the Hertfordshire Witchcraft consider'd. Being an Examination of a Book, entitl'd, A Full and Impartial Account [etc.]; (3) The Impossibility of Witchcraft . . . In which the Depositions against Jane Wenham . . . are Confuted and Expos'd; (4) The Belief of Witchcraft Vindicated . . . in Answer to a late Pamphlet, Intituled, The Impossibility of Witchcraft. By G. R. A. M.; (5) A Defense of the Proceedings against Jane Wenham. By Francis Bragge; (6) Witchcraft Farther Display'd; (7) A Full Confutation of Witchcraft: more particularly of the Depositions against Jane Wenham . . . In a Letter from a Physician in Hertfordshire, to his Friend in London. The first and fifth of these pamphlets are by Bragge, a Cambridge graduate who gave evidence for the prosecution. See also Memoirs of Literature, London, 1722, IV, 357; Wright, Narratives of Sorcery and Witchcraft, II, 319 ff. Jane Wenham lived nearly twenty years after her trial; she died in 1730 (Clutterbuck, History and Antiquities of the County of Hertford, II, 461; W. B. Gerish, A Hertfordshire Witch, p. 10).

[130] I refer to such remarks as the following:—" As the devil lost his empire among us in the last age, he exercised it with greater violence among the Indian Pawwaws, and our New England colonists" (Richard Gough, British Topography, 1780, II.

Yet Thomas Wright—never to be mentioned without honor— speaks of the New England troubles as "exemplifying the horrors and the absurdities of the witchcraft persecutions more than anything that had occurred in the old world,"[181] and Dr. G. H. Moore,—in an important article on The Bibliography of Witchcraft in Massachusetts—declares that the Salem outbreak "was the *epitome* of witchcraft! whose ghastly records may be challenged to produce any parallel for it in the world's history!"[182]  In further refutation of such reckless statements I need add but a single instance.  In 1596 there was an outbreak of some pestilence or other in Aberdeen.  The populace ascribed the disease to the machinations of a family long suspected of witchcraft.  A special commission was appointed by the Privy Council, "and before April 1597, twenty-three women and one man had been burnt, one woman had died under the torture, one had hanged herself in prison, and four others who were acquitted on the capital charge, were yet branded on the cheek and banished from the sheriffdom."[183]

There was a very special reason why troubles with the powers of darkness were to be expected in New England,— a reason which does not hold good for Great Britain or, indeed, for any part of Western Europe.  I refer, of course, to the presence of a considerable heathen population—the Indians.  These were universally supposed to be devil-

---

254, note ⁹); "The colonists of [Massachusetts] appear to have carried with them, in an exaggerated form, the superstitious feelings with regard to witchcraft which then [at the time of the settlement] prevailed in the mother country" (Introduction to the reprint of Cotton Mather's Wonders of the Invisible World, in the Library of Old Authors, 1862); "In the dark and dangerous forests of America the animistic instinct, the original source of the superstition, operated so powerfully in Puritan minds that Cotton Mather's *Wonders of the Invisible World* and the Salem persecution surpassed in credulity and malignity anything the mother country could show" (Ferris Greenslet, Joseph Glanvill, New York, 1900, pp. 150-151); "The new world, from the time of its settlement, has been a kind of health resort for the worn-out delusions of the old . . . For years prior to the Salem excitement, European witchcraft had been prostrate on its dying bed, under the watchful and apprehensive eyes of religion and of law; carried over the ocean it arose to its feet, and threatened to depopulate New England" (George M. Beard, The Psychology of the Salem Witchcraft Excitement, New York, 1882, p. 1).

[181] Narratives of Sorcery and Magic, II, 284.

[182] Proceedings American Antiquarian Society, New Series, V, 267.

[183] F. Legge, Witchcraft in Scotland, in The Scottish Review, October, 1891, XVIII, 263.

worshippers—not only by the Colonists but by all the rest of the world—for paganism was held to be nothing but Satanism.[184] Cotton Mather and the Jesuit fathers of Canada were at one on this point.[185] The religious ceremonies of the Indians were, as we know, in large part an invocation of spirits, and their powwows, or medicine men, supposed themselves to be wizards,—*were* wizards, indeed, so far as sorcery is possible.[186] The Colonial government showed itself singularly moderate, however, in its attitude toward Indian practices of a magical character. Powwowing was, of course, forbidden wherever the jurisdiction of the white men held sway, but it was punishable by fine only, nor was there any idea of inflicting the extreme penalty[187]—although the offence undoubtedly came under the Mosaic law, so often quoted on the title-pages of books on witchcraft, "Thou shalt not suffer a witch to live."

The existence of all these devil-worshipping neighbors was a constant reminder of the possibility of danger from witchcraft. One is surprised, therefore, to find that there was no real outbreak until so late in the century. It argues an uncommon degree of steadiness and common sense among our forefathers that they held off the explosion so long. Yet even this delay has been made to count against them, as if, by 1692, they ought to have known better,

[184] On modern savages as devil worshippers, see, for example, Henry More, Divine Dialogues, 1668, I, 404 ff. (Dialogue iii, sections 15-16).

[185] Magnalia, book i, chap. i, §2, ed. 1853, I, 42; book, vi, chap. vi, §3, III, 436; Jesuit Relations, ed. Thwaites, I, 286; II, 76; VIII, 124, 126. See also Thomas Morton, New English Canaan, 1637, chap. ix, ed. Adams, (Prince Society), p. 150, with the references in Mr. Adams's note. Cf. Hutchinson, History of Massachusetts, chap. vi, ed. 1795, I, 419 ff.; Diary of Ezra Stiles, June 13, 1773, ed. Dexter, I, 385-386.

[186] Mayhew's letter of Oct. 22, 1652, in Eliot and Mayhew's Tears of Repentance, 1653 (Mass. Hist. Soc. Collections, 3d Series, IV, 203-206); Gookin, Historical Collections of the Indians in New England (Mass. Hist. Soc. Collections, I, 154). See the references in Mr. Adams's note to Morton's New English Canaan, Prince Society edition, p. 152, and compare the following places in the Eliot Tracts (as reprinted in the Mass. Hist. Soc. Collections, 3d Series, IV), —pp. 17, 19-20, 39, 50-51, 55-57, 77, 82, 113-116, 133-134, 156, 186-187. See, for the impression that Indian ceremonies made on a devout man in 1745, David Brainerd's Journal, Mirabilia Dei inter Indicos, Philadelphia, [1746,] pp. 49-57:—"I sat," writes Brainerd, "at a small Distance, not more than Thirty Feet from them, (tho' undiscover'd) with my Bible in my Hand, resolving if possible to spoil their Sport, and prevent their receiving any Answers from the *infernal* world" (p. 50).

[187] Gookin, Historical Collections (Mass. Hist. Soc. Collections, I, 154); Mass. Records, ed. Shurtleff, II, 177; III, 98.

even if they might have been excusable some years before. In point of fact, the New Englanders, as we have seen, made an end of trying witches nearly ten years earlier than their English fellow-citizens. But we shall come back to this question of dates presently.

Much has been written of the stupendous and criminal foolishness of our ancestors in admitting "spectral evidence" at the Salem trials. Nothing, of course, can be said in defence of such evidence in itself; but a great deal might be said in defence of our ancestors on this score. The fact is,—and it should never be lost sight of,—there was nothing strange in their admitting such evidence. It was a matter of course that they should admit it. To do so indeed, was one of the best established of all legal principles. Spectral evidence was admitted, for example, in England, either in examinations or in actual trials, in 1593,[138] 1612,[139] 1616,[140] 1621,[141] 1633,[142] 1645,[143] 1650,[144] 1653,[145] 1654,[146] 1658,[147] 1660,[148] 1661,[149] 1663,[150] 1664,[151] 1665,[152] 1667,[153] 1670,[154]

[138] The Most Strange and Admirable Discoverie of the Three Witches of Warboys, 1593, sig. B2 r°, P v°.

[139] Thomas Potts, The Wonderfull Discoverie of Witches, 1613 (Chetham Society reprint, sig. 8); The Arraignment and Triall of Iennet Preston, of Gisborne in Craven, in the Countie of York, London, 1612 (in same reprint, sig. Y 2).

[140] Mary Smith's case, Alexander Roberts, A Treatise of Witchcraft, 1616, pp. 52, 56, 57; the Husband's Bosworth case, Letter of Alderman Robert Heyrick, of Leicester, July 18, 1616, printed in Nichols, History and Antiquities of the County of Leicester, II, 471*.

[141] Edward Fairfax, Dæmonologia, 1621 (first edited by W. Grainge, Harrogate, 1882).

[142] Chetham Society Publications, V, lxiv.

[143] A True and Exact Relation of the Severall Informations, [etc.] of the late Witches, London, 1645, p. 20; T. B. Howell, State Trials, IV, 846.

[144] Depositions from the Castle of York, [edited by James Raine,] Surtees Society, 1861 (Publications, XL), pp. 28-30.

[145] The same, p. 58.

[146] The same, pp. 64-65, 67.

[147] Glanvill, Saducismus Triumphatus, ed. 1682, Relations, pp. 96, 98, 100 (ed. 1726, pp. 286, 288, 289).

[148] York Depositions, p. 82.

[149] The same, pp. 88-89, 92.

[150] The same, pp. 112-114; Glanvill, ed. 1682, pp. 160-161 (ed. 1726, pp. 328-329).

[151] A Tryal of Witches . . . at Bury St. Edmonds . . . 1664, London, 1682, pp. 18, 20, 23, 26, 29, 34, 38 (Sir Matthew Hale's case); York Depositions, pp. 124-125.

[152] Glanvill, ed. 1682, pp. 103-104, 109 (ed. 1726, p. 291).

[153] Calendar of State Papers, Domestic Series, 1667-1668, p. 4; York Depositions, p. 154.

[154] York Depositions, p. 176.

1672,[155] 1673,[156] 1680,[157] 1683.[158] Even Chief Justice Holt, whose honorable record in procuring the acquittal of every witch he tried is well-known,[159] did not exclude spectral evidence: it was offered and admitted in at least two of his cases—in 1695 and 1696[160]—both later than the last witch trial in Massachusetts. In the 1697 edition of that very popular manual, Michael Dalton's Country Justice, spectral evidence ("Their Apparition to the Sick Party in his Fits") is expressly mentioned as one of the proofs of witchcraft.[161] What may fairly be called spectral evidence was admitted by Mr. Justice Powell, anxious as he was to have the defendant acquitted, in the trial of Jane Wenham in 1712.[162] The question, then, was not whether such evidence might be heard, but what weight was to be attached to it. Thus, in Sir Matthew Hale's case, Mr. Serjeant Keeling was "much unsatisfied" with such testimony, affirming that, if it were allowed to

[155] Ann Tilling's case, Gentleman's Magazine for 1832, Part I, CII, 489 ff.; Inderwick, Side-Lights on the Stuarts, 2d ed., 1891, pp. 171-172, 191.

[156] York Depositions, pp. 192, 202-203.

[157] The same, p. 247.

[158] Margaret Stothard's case, The Monthly Chronicle of North-Country Lore and Legend, [II] 1888, p. 395.

[159] See page 54.

[160] F. Hutchinson, Historical Essay, 1718, pp. 44-45 (ed. 1720, pp. 61-62). There is a very interesting account of the second of these trials (that of Elizabeth Horner or Turner) in a letter to the Bishop of Exeter from Archdeacon (?) Blackburne, who attended at the bishop's request. This letter, dated Sept. 14, 1696, has been printed by Mr. T. Quiller-Couch in Notes and Queries, 1st Series, XI, 498-499, and again in Brand's Popular Antiquities, ed. Hazlitt, III, 103-104. The spectral evidence comes out clearly. Of Holt, Blackburne remarks: "My Lord Chief Justice by his questions and manner of summing up the Evidence seem'd to me to believe nothing of witchery at all."

[161] Chap. 160, sec. 5, p. 384. "The court justified themselves from books of law, and the authorities of Keble, Dalton and other lawyers, then of the first character, who lay down rules of conviction as absurd and dangerous, as any which were practiced in New England." Hutchinson, History of Massachusetts, ed. 1795, II, 27.

[162] James Burvile testified "That hearing the Scratchings and Noises of Cats, he went out, and saw several of them; that one of them had a Face like Jane Wenham; that he was present several Times when Anne Thorn said she saw Cats about her Bed; and more he would have attested, but this was thought sufficient by the Court" ([F. Bragge,] A Full and Impartial Account of the Discovery of Sorcery and Witchcraft, practis'd by Jane Wenham, London, 1712, p. 29). After the conviction of the witch, Ann was still afflicted: "Ann Thorn continues to be frequently troubl'd with the Apparition either of Jane Wenham in her own Shape, or that of a Cat, which speaks to her, and tempts her to destroy her self with a Knife that it brings along with it" ([Bragge,] Witchcraft Farther Display'd, 1712, Introduction). In 1711 spectral evidence was admitted at the trial of eight witches at Carrickfergus, in Ireland (A Narrative of some Strange Events that took place in Island Magee, and Neighbourhood, in 1711, by an Eye Witness, Belfast, 1822, Appendix, pp. 49-50).

pass for proof, ''no person whatsoever can be in safety.''[163]
He did not aver that it should not have been admitted,
but only protested against regarding it as decisive, and in
the end he seems to have become convinced of the guilt
of the defendants.[164] It is, therefore, nothing against
our ancestors that they heard such evidence, for they were
simply following the invariable practice of the English
courts. On the other hand, it is much to their credit that
they soon began to suspect it, and that, having taken advice,
they decided, in 1693, to allow it no further weight. We
may emphasize the folly of spectral evidence as much as
we like.[165] Only let us remember that in so doing we are
attacking, not New England in 1692, but Old England
from 1593 to 1712. When, on the other hand, we distribute
compliments to those who refused to allow such evidence
to constitute full proof, let us not forget that with the name
of Chief Justice Holt we must associate those of certain
Massachusetts worthies whom I need not specify. It is
not permissible to blame our ancestors for an error of
judgment that they shared with everybody, and then to
refuse them commendation for a virtue which they shared
with a very few wise heads in England. That would be
to proceed on the principle of ''heads I win, tails you lose,''—
a method much followed by Matthew Hopkins and his
kind, but of doubtful propriety in a candid investigation
of the past. We shall never keep our minds clear on the
question of witchcraft in general, and of the Salem witchcraft in particular, until we stop attacking and defending
individual persons.

Sir John Holt, Chief Justice of the King's Bench from
1682 to 1710, has a highly honorable name in the annals
of English witchcraft. A dozen or twenty cases came before
him, and in every instance the result was an acquittal.[166]

---

[163] A Tryal of Witches, as above, p. 40.

[164] "The Judge and all the Court were fully satisfied with the Verdict" (A Tryal,
etc., p. 58).

[165] For a learned discussion of spectral evidence see J. B. Thayer, Atlantic Monthly,
April, 1890, LXV, 471 ff.

[166] Dr. Hutchinson, who acknowledges his indebtedness to Holt, mentions six
witches as tried by the Chief Justice from 1691 to 1696, and adds, "Several others
in other Places, about Eleven in all, have been tried for Witches before my

Chief Justice Holt deserves all the credit he has received; but it must be carefully noted that his example cannot be cited to the shame and confusion of our ancestors in Massachusetts, for most of his cases,—all but one, so far as I can ascertain,—occurred after the release of the New England prisoners and the abandonment of the prosecution here. As to that single case of acquittal, we must not forget that there were also acquittals in New England,— in 1674 and 1676, for example.[167] As to acquittals in England *after* 1693, let it be remembered that there were *no trials at all for witchcraft* in New England subsequent to that year. If Chief Justice Holt is to be commended for procuring the acquittal of a dozen witches between 1693 and 1702, what is to be ascribed to our forefathers for bringing no cases to trial during that period?

The most remarkable things about the New England prosecution were the rapid return of the community to its habitually sensible frame of mind and the frank public confession of error made by many of those who had been implicated. These two features, and especially the latter, are without a parallel in the history of witchcraft. It seems to be assumed by most writers that recantation and an appeal to heaven for pardon were the least that could have been expected of judge and jury. In fact, as I have just ventured to suggest, no action like Samuel Sewall's on the part of a judge and no document like that issued by the repentant Massachusetts jurymen have yet been discovered in the witch records of the world.[168]

---

Lord Chief Justice *Holt*, and have all been acquitted. The last of them was *Sarah Morduck*, accused by *Richard Hathaway*, and tried at *Guilford* Assize, *Anno* 1701" (Historical Essay, 2d ed., pp. 58-63). It is not clear whether the "eleven in all" includes the seven previously mentioned. On the Morduck-Hathaway case, cf. Howell, State Trials, XIV, 639 ff.

[167] Drake, Annals of Witchcraft in New England, pp. 136, 138.

[168] Compare Mr. Goodell's remarks on the reversal of attainder, in his Reasons for Concluding that the Act of 1711 became a Law, 1884. I have not considered here the bearing of this reversal, or of the attempt to pay damages to the survivors or their heirs, because these things came somewhat later. It must be noted, however, that all such measures of reparation, whatever may be thought of their sufficiency, were unexampled in the history of witch trials the world over, and that they came before the last condemnation for witchcraft in England (1712). See the references appended by Mr. Goodell to the Act of 1703 in The Acts and Resolves of the Province of the Massachusetts Bay, VI, 49-50.

But it is not for the sake of lauding their penitential exercises that I lay stress upon the unexampled character of our forefathers' action. There is another aspect from which the outcome of the Salem trials ought to be regarded. They fell at a critical moment, when witchcraft was, for whatever reason, soon to become a crime unknown to the English courts. They attracted attention instantly in the Mother Country.[169] Can there be any question that the sensational recovery of the Province from its attack of prosecuting zeal, accompanied as that recovery was by retraction and by utterances of deep contrition, had a profound effect in England? The mere dropping of the prosecution would not have had this effect. In 1597, James I., alarmed at the extent to which witch trials were going in Scotland, revoked all the existing special commissions that were engaged in holding trials for this offence.[170] But the evil was soon worse than ever. What was efficacious in the New England instance was the unheard-of action of judge and jury in recanting. This made the Salem troubles the best argument conceivable in the hands of those reformers who, soon after 1700, began to make actual headway in their opposition to the witch dogma.

I am not reasoning *a priori*. By common consent one of the most effective arraignments of the superstition that we are discussing is the Historical Essay on Witchcraft of Dr. Francis Hutchinson, which appeared in 1718.[171] Now Hutchinson, who gives much space to the New England trials, refers to Sewall's action, and prints the recantation of the jurors in full. Nor does he leave in us doubt as to the purpose for which he adduces these testimonies. "And those Towns," he writes, "having regained their Quiet; and this Case being of that Nature, that Facts and Experience are of more weight than meer rational Arguments; it will be worth our while to observe some Passages that happened after this Storm, when they had Time to look back on what had passed."[172]

---

[169] See p. 17, above.
[170] Legge, as above, p. 264.
[171] 2d ed., 1720.
[172] P. 83; 2d ed., p. 108.

Whatever may be thought of these considerations, one fact cannot be assailed. In prosecuting witches, our forefathers acted like other men in the seventeenth century. In repenting and making public confession, they acted like themselves. Their fault was the fault of their time; their merit is their own.

We must not leave this subject without looking into the question of numbers and dates. The history of the Salem Witchcraft is, to all intents and purposes, the sum total of witchcraft history in the whole of Massachusetts for a century. From the settlement of the country, of course, our fathers believed in witchcraft, and cases came before the courts from time to time, but, outside of the Salem outbreak, not more than half-a-dozen executions can be shown to have occurred. It is not strange that there should have been witch trials. It is inconceivable that the Colony should have passed through its first century without some special outbreak of prosecution—inconceivable, that is to say, to one who knows what went on in England and the rest of Europe during that time. The wonderful thing is, not that an outbreak of prosecution occurred, but that it did not come sooner and last longer.

From the first pranks of the afflicted children in Mr. Parris's house (in February, 1692) to the collapse of the prosecution in January, 1693, was less than a year. During the interval twenty persons had suffered death, and two are known to have died in jail.[178] If to these we add the six sporadic cases that occurred in Massachusetts before 1692, there is a total of twenty-eight; but this is the whole reckoning, not merely for a year or two but for a complete century. The concentration of the trouble in Massachusetts within the limits of a single year has given a wrong turn to the thoughts of many writers. This concentration makes the case more conspicuous, but it does not make

---

[178] See W. F. Poole, in Winsor's Memorial History of Boston, II, 133. Dr. Poole finds twelve executions in New England before 1692. This makes the total for all New England, from 1620 to the present day, 34 (including two who died in jail). Cf. C. W. Upham, Salem Witchcraft, Boston, 1867, II, 351; S. G. Drake, Annals of Witchcraft, pp. 191 ff. In this part of my paper I have made a few quotations from a book of my own, The Old Farmer and his Almanack (Boston, 1904).

it worse. On the contrary, it makes it better. It is astonishing that there should have been only half-a-dozen executions for witchcraft in Massachusetts before 1692, and equally astonishing that the delusion, when it became acute, should have raged for but a year, and that but twenty-two persons should have lost their lives. The facts are distinctly creditable to our ancestors,—to their moderation and . to the rapidity with which their good sense could reassert itself after a brief eclipse.[174]

Let us compare figures a little. For Massachusetts the account is simple—twenty-eight victims in a century. No one has ever made an accurate count of the executions in England during the seventeenth century, but they must have mounted into the hundreds.[175] Matthew Hopkins, the Witch-finder General, brought at least two hundred to the gallows from 1645 to 1647.[176] In Scotland

---

[174] "They were the first of all people," writes Mr. Goodell, "to escape the thraldom" (Reasons for Concluding that the Act of 1711 became a Law, 1884, p. 21).

[175] See Francis Hutchinson, Historical Essay, 2d edition, 1720, pp. 45 ff.

[176] John Stearne, Hopkins's associate, speaks of what he has himself "learned and observed since the 25. of March 1645 as being in part an agent in finding out or discovering some of those since that time, being about two hundred in number, in Essex, Suffolke, Northamptonshire, Huntingtonshire, Bedfordshire, Norfolke, Cambridgeshire, and the Isle of Ely in the County of Cambridge, besides other places, justly and deservedly executed upon their legall tryalls" (A Confirmation and Discovery of Witch-craft, London, 1648, To the Reader). Stearne wrote his book after the death of Hopkins, which took place in 1647. In the life of Hopkins in the Dictionary of National Biography, the Witch-Finder is said to have begun operations in 1644. This is a manifest error. Hopkins himself (Discovery of Witches, 1647, p. 2, see below) says that his experiences began at Manningtree "in March 1644," but Stearne's statement makes it clear that this is Old Style, for Stearne was also concerned in the Manningtree business, and the year is completely established by the report of the proceedings,—A True and Exact Relation of the several Informations [etc.] of the late Witches, London, 1645 (cf. T. B. Howell's State Trials, IV, 817 ff.). The traditional statement that Hopkins was hanged as a wizard (cf. Hudibras, Part ii, canto 3, ll. 139 ff.) is disproved by the following passage in Stearne: "I am certain (notwithstanding whatsoever hath been said of him) he died peaceably at Manningtree, after a long sickness of a Consumption, as many of his generation had done before him, without any trouble of conscience for what he had done, as was falsly reported of him" (p. 61). For the record of his burial, Aug. 12, 1647, see Notes and Queries, 1st Series, X, 285. The notion that Hopkins was "swum" and, since he floated, was subsequently hanged, most likely originated in a document criticising his performances which was brought before the Norfolk judges in 1646 or (more probably) in 1647. Hopkins printed a reply to this document shortly before his death,—The Discovery of Witches: in Answer to severall Queries, lately delivered to the Judges of Assize for the County of Norfolk. And now published by Matthew Hopkins, Witch-finder (London, 1647). The first "query," as printed by Hopkins, was this:—"That he must needs be the greatest Witch, Sorcerer, and Wizzard himselfe, else hee could not doe it." Cf. Wright, Narratives of Sorcery and Magic, II, 145 ff.;

the number of victims was much larger. The most conscientiously moderate estimate makes out a total of at least 3,400 between the years 1580 and 1680, and the computer declares that future discoveries in the way of records may force us to increase this figure very much.[177] On the Continent many thousands suffered death in the sixteenth and seventeenth centuries. Mannhardt reckons the victims from the fourteenth to the seventeenth century at millions,[178] and half a million is thought to be a moderate estimate. In Alsace, a hundred and thirty-four witches and wizards were burned in 1582 on one occasion, the execution taking place on the 15th, 19th, 24th, and 28th of October.[179] Nicholas Remy (Remigius) of Lorraine gathered the materials for his work on the Worship of Demons,[180] published in 1595, from the trials of some 900 persons whom he had sentenced to death in the fifteen years preceding. In 1609, de Lancre and his associate are said to have condemned 700 in the Basque country in four months.[181] The efforts of the Bishop of Bamberg from 1622 to 1633 resulted in six hundred executions; the Bishop of Würzburg, in about the same period, put nine hundred persons to death.[182] These figures, which might be multiplied almost indefinitely,[188] help us to look at the Salem Witchcraft in its true proportions,—

---

Lives of Twelve Bad Men, edited by Thomas Seccombe, London, 1894, p. 64; Ady, A Candle in the Dark, 1656, pp. 101-102; James Howell, as above (p. 8, note 7); Gough, British Topography, 1780, II, 254.

[177] Legge, Scottish Review, XVIII, 273-274. Ady (A Candle in the Dark, 1656, p. 105) says: "A little before the Conquest of Scotland (as is reported upon good intelligence) the Presbytery of Scotland did, by their own pretended authority, take upon them to Summon, Convent, Censure, and Condemn people to cruel death for Witches and ( as is credibly reported) they caused four thousand to be executed by Fire and Halter, and had as many in prison to be tried by them, when God sent his conquering Sword to suppress them." The "conquest" to which Ady refers is Cromwell's, in 1650. It is well known that from 1640 to Cromwell's invasion, witch prosecution ran riot in Scotland, but that during his supremacy there were very few executions in that country (see Legge, pp. 266-267). Cf. p. 8, note 6, above.

[178] Die praktischen Folgen des Aberglaubens, p. 34.

[179] Soldan, Geschichte der Hexenprozesse, ed. Heppe, I, 492.

[180] Dæmonolatreia, Lugduni, 1595.

[181] See p. 42, above.

[182] Soldan, Geschichte der Hexenprozesse, ed. Heppe, II, 38 ff.

[188] See the extraordinary enumeration in Roskoff, Geschichte des Teufels, Leipzig, 1869, II, 293 ff.; cf. S. Riezler, Geschichte der Hexenprozesse in Bayern, pp. 141 ff., 283 ff.

as a very small incident in the history of a terrible superstition.

These figures may perhaps be attacked as involving a fallacious comparison, inasmuch as we have not attempted to make the relative population of New England and the several districts referred to a factor in the equation. Such an objection, if anybody should see fit to make it, is easily answered by other figures. The total number of victims in Massachusetts from the first settlement to the end of the seventeenth century was, as we have seen, twenty-eight, —or thirty-four for the whole of New England. Compare the following figures, taken from the annals of Great Britain and Scotland alone. In 1612, ten witches were executed belonging to a single district of Lancashire.[184] In 1645 twenty-nine witches were condemned at once in a single Hundred in Essex,[185] eighteen were hanged at once at Bury in Suffolk[186] "and a hundred and twenty more were to have been tried, but a sudden movement of the king's troops in that direction obliged the judges to adjourn the session.[187] Under date of July 26, 1645, Whitelocke records that "20 Witches in Norfolk were executed,"[188] and again, under April 15, 1650, that "at a little Village within two Miles [of Berwick] two Men and three Women were burnt for Witches, and nine more were to be burnt, the Village consisting of but fourteen Families, and there were as many witches" and further that "twenty more were to be burnt within six Miles of that place."[189] If we pass over to the Continent, the numbers are appalling. Whether, then, we take the computation in gross or in detail, New England emerges from the test with credit.

The last execution for witchcraft in Massachusetts took place in 1692, as we have seen; indeed, twenty of the total of twenty-six cases fell within the limits of that one year. There were no witch trials in New England in the

---

[184] Potts, The Wonderfull Discoverie of Witches, 1613 (Chetham Society reprint).
[185] Matthew Hopkins, Discovery of Witches, 1647, p. 3.
[186] John Stearne, A Confirmation and Discovery of Witchcraft, 1648, p. 14.
[187] Wright, Narratives of Sorcery and Magic, Chap. xxv.
[188] Memorials, 1732, p. 163.
[189] Page 450.

eighteenth century. The annals of Europe are not so clear. Six witches were burned in Renfrewshire in 1697.[190] In England, Elinor Shaw and Mary Phillips, "two notorious witches," were put to death at Northampton in 1705 (or 1706).[191] In 1712 Jane Wenham was condemned to death for witchcraft, but she was pardoned.[192] Two clergymen of the Church of England, as well as a Bachelor of Arts of Cambridge,[193] gave evidence against her. Just before the arrest of Jane Wenham, Addison in the Spectator for July 11, 1711, had expressed the creed of a well-bred and sensible man of the world: "I believe in general that there is, and has been such a thing as Witchcraft; but at the same time can give no Credit to any particular Instance of it." Blackstone, it will be remembered, subscribed to the same doctrine, making particular reference to Addison.[194]

---

[190] A Relation of the Diabolical Practices of above Twenty Wizards and Witches, 1697; Sadducismus Debellatus, 1698; A History of the Witches of Renfrewshire, 1877. A seventh committed suicide in prison.

[191] An Account of the Tryals, Examination and Condemnation, of Elinor Shaw, and Mary Phillips [etc.], London [1705]; The Northamptonshire Witches. Being a true and faithful Account of the Births [etc.] of Elinor Shaw, and Mary Phillips, (The two notorious Witches) That were executed at Northampton on Saturday, March the 17th, 1705 . . . Communicated in a Letter last Post, from Mr. Ralph Davis, of Northampton . . . London, 1705. The first tract is dated March 8, 1705; the second, March 18th, 1705. Both are signed "Ralph Davis." I have used the reprints by Taylor & Son, Northampton, 1866. On this case, see [ F. Marshall,] A Brief History of Witchcraft, with Especial Reference to Northamptonshire, Northampton, 1866, pp. 13-15, 16; Notes and Queries, 7th Series, IX, 117; Northamptonshire Notes and Queries II, 19; Eugene Teesdale, in Bygone Northamptonshire, edited by William Andrews, 1891, pp. 114-115; Gough, British Topography, 1780, II, 46.

[192] See p. 48, above. This was the last conviction for witchcraft, and probably the last trial, in England. Mrs. Mary Hickes and her daughter are said by Gough (British Topography, 1780, I, 439, II, 254, note) to have been executed for witchcraft on July 28, 1716, at Huntingdon. Gough cites a contemporary pamphlet as authority. The genuineness of this case is doubted (see Notes and Queries, 1st Series, V, 514; 2d Series, V, 503-504), but Mr. F. A. Inderwick argues for its acceptance (Side-Lights on the Stuarts, 2d ed., 1891, pp. 177-180), and it has certainly never been disproved. The alleged executions at Northampton in 1712 are certainly based on a slip of the pen in Gough, British Topography, 1780, II, 52; the cases actually occurred in 1612, and an account of them may be found in a tract (The Witches of Northamptonshire) published in that year, and reprinted by Taylor & Son, Northampton, 1867. See also Thomas Sternberg, The Dialect and Folk-Lore of Northamptonshire, London, 1851, p. 152; F. Marshall, A Brief History of Witchcraft, Northampton, 1866, p. 16.

[193] That is, Francis Bragge, who was also a clergyman, being Curate of Biggleswade according to Mr. W. B. Gerish (A Hertfordshire Witch, p. 8).

[194] Commentaries, book iv, chap. 4, sec. 6 (4th ed., 1770, IV, 60-61); cf. Dr. Samuel A. Green, Groton in the Witchcraft Times, 1883, p. 29. In 1715 and 1716 there appeared, in London, A Compleat History of Magick, Sorcery, and Witchcraft, in

Prompted, one may conjecture, by the stir which the Wenham trial made, the Rev. J. Boys, of Coggeshall Magna, in Essex, transcribed, in this same year, from his memoranda, A Brief Account of the Indisposition of the Widow Coman. This case had occurred in his own parish in 1699, and he had given it careful investigation. Both in 1699, when he jotted down the facts, and in 1712, Mr. Boys was clearly of the opinion that his unfortunate parishioner was a witch. His narrative, which remained in manuscript until 1901,[195] may be profitably compared with Cotton Mather's account of his visit to Margaret Rule in 1693.[196] Such a comparison will not work to the disadvantage of the New England divine. Incidentally it may be mentioned that the mob ''swam'' the widow Coman several times, and that ''soon after, whether by the cold she got in the water or by some other means, she fell very ill, and dyed.'' Let it not be forgotten that this was six years after the end of the witchcraft prosecutions in Massachusetts. In 1705 a supposed witch was murdered by a mob at Pittenween in Scotland.[197] In 1730, another alleged witch succumbed to the water ordeal in Somersetshire.[198] The English and Scottish statutes against witchcraft were repealed in 1736,[199] but in that same year Joseph

---

two volumes, which asserted the truth, and gave the particulars, of a long line of such phenomena, from the case of the Witches of Warboys (in 1592) to the Salem Witchcraft itself. The book was the occasion of Dr. Francis Hutchinson's Historical Essay, published in 1718, and in a second edition in 1720. Richard Boulton, the author of the Compleat History, returned to the charge in 1722, in The Possibility and Reality of Magick, Sorcery, and Witchcraft, Demonstrated. Or, a Vindication of a Compleat History of Magick, etc. The Compleat History came out anonymously, but Boulton, who describes himself as "sometime of Brazen-Nose College in Oxford," acknowledges the authorship in his reply to Hutchinson.

[195] The Case of Witchcraft at Coggeshall, Essex, in the year, 1699, being the Narrative of the Rev. J. Boys, Minister of that Parish. Printed from his Manuscript in the possession of the Publisher. London, A. Russell Smith, 1901 (50 copies only).

[196] In Calef, More Wonders of the Invisible World, 1700, pp. 3 ff.

[197] An Answer of a Letter from a Gentleman in Fife, 1705; cf. also A Collection of Rare and Curious Tracts on Witchcraft and the Second Sight, Edinburgh, 1820, pp. 79 ff.

[198] Daily Journal, Jan 15, 1731, as quoted in the Gentleman's Magazine for 1731, I, 29.

[199] Daines Barrington points with pride to this early abolition of penalties:— "It is greatly to the honour of this country, to have repealed all the statutes against this supposed crime so long ago as the year 1736, when laws of the same sort continue in full force against these miserable and aged objects of compassion, in every other part of Europe" (Observations on the More Ancient Statutes, 3d ed., 1769, p. 367, on 20 Henr. VI.).

63

Juxson, vicar, preached at Twyford, in Leicestershire, a
Sermon upon Witchcraft, occasioned by a late Illegal
Attempt to discover Witches by Swimming,[200] and in 1751
Ruth Osborne, a reputed witch, was murdered by a mob
in Hertfordshire.[201] The last execution for witchcraft
in Germany took place in 1775. In Spain the last witch
was burned in 1781. In Switzerland Anna Göldi was
beheaded in 1782 for bewitching the child of her master,
a physician. In Poland two women were burned as late
as 1793.[202]

That the belief in witchcraft is still pervasive among the
peasantry of Europe, and to a considerable extent among
the foreign-born population in this country, is a matter of
common knowledge.[203] Besides, spiritualism and kindred
delusions have taken over, under changed names, many
of the phenomena, real and pretended, which would have
been explained as due to witchcraft in days gone by.[204]

Why did the Salem outbreak occur? Of course there
were many causes—some of which have already suggested
themselves in the course of our discussion. But one fact
should be borne in mind as of particular importance. The

---

[200] Gough, British Topography, 1780, I, 517.
[201] Gentleman's Magazine for 1751, XXI, 186, 198; Wright, Narratives of Sorcery
and Magic, II, 326 ff.; Gough, as above, I, 431.
[202] Soldan, ed. Heppe, II, 314, 322, 327.
[203] See, for example, A. Löwenstimm, Aberglaube und Strafrecht, Berlin, 1897;
W. Mannhardt, Die praktischen Folgen des Aberglaubens, 1878 (Deutsche Zeit-und
Streit-Fragen, ed. by F. von Holstendorff, VII, nos. 97, 98); Wuttke, Der Deutsche
Volksaberglaube der Gegenwart, 2d ed., 1869; the chapter on Hexerei und Hexen-
verfolgung im neunzehnten Jahrhundert, in Soldan, Geschichte der Hexenprozesse,
ed. by Heppe, II, 330 ff; cf. The Monthly Chronicle of North-Country Lore and
Legend, [II.] 1888, p. 394; North Riding Record Society, Publications, IV, 20,
note; History of Witchcraft, sketched from the Popular Tales of the Peasantry of
Nithsdale and Galloway (R. H. Cromek, Remains of Nithsdale and Galloway Song,
1810, pp. 272 ff.); H. M. Doughty, Blackwood's Magazine, March, 1898, CLXIII,
394-395; Brand's Popular Antiquities, ed. Hazlitt, III, 71, 95, 96, 100 ff.; The Anti-
quary, XLI, 363; W. G. Black, Folk-Medicine, 1883; Miss Burne, Shropshire Folk-
Lore, Chap. xiii; W. Henderson, Notes on the Folk-Lore of the Northern Counties,
1879, Chap. vi; J. G. Campbell, Witchcraft and Second Sight in the Highlands and
Islands of Scotland, 1902; Notes and Queries, 1st Series, VII, 613, XI, 497-498;
3rd Series, II, 325; 4th Series, III, 238, VII, 53, VIII, 44; 5th Series, V, 126, 223,
IX, 433, X, 205, XI, 66; 6th Series, I, 19, II, 145, IV, 510; 7th Series, IX, 425, XI,
43; 8th Series, IV, 186, 192, V, 226, VI, 6, VII, 246; 9th Series, II, 466, XII, 187; the
journal, Folk-Lore, passim.
[204] Cf. Allen Putnam, Witchcraft of New England explained by Modern Spiritualism, Boston, 1880.

belief in witchcraft, as we have already had occasion to
remark, was a constant quantity; but outbreaks of prosecution came, in England—and, generally speaking, elsewhere
—spasmodically, at irregular intervals. If we look at Great
Britain for a moment, we shall see that such outbreaks
are likely to coincide with times of political excitement
or anxiety. Thus early in Elizabeth's reign, when everything was more or less unsettled, Bishop Jewel, whom all
historians delight to honor, made a deliberate and avowed
digression, in a sermon before the queen, in order to warn
her that witchcraft was rampant in the realm, to inform
her (on the evidence of his own eyes) that her subjects
were being injured in their goods and their health, and
to exhort her to enforce the law.[205] The initial zeal of
James I. in the prosecution of witches stood in close connection with the trouble he was having with his turbulent
cousin Francis Bothwell.[206] The operations of Matthew
Hopkins (in 1645-1647) were a mere accompaniment to
the tumult of the Civil War; the year in which they began
was the year of Laud's execution and of the Battle of
Naseby. The Restoration was followed by a fresh outbreak of witch prosecution,—mild in England, though
far-reaching in its consequences, but very sharp in Scotland.

With facts like these in view, we can hardly regard it
as an accident that the Salem witchcraft marks a time

---

[205] "And by the way, to touch but a word or two of this matter, for that the horrible vsing of your poore subiects inforceth thereunto: It may please your Grace
to vnderstand, that this kind of people, I meane witches, and sorcerers, within these
few last yeeres, are maruellously increased within this your Graces realme. These eies
haue seene most euident and manifest marks of their wickednesse. Your Graces
subiects pine away euen vnto death, their collour fadeth, their flesh rotteth, their
speech is benummed, their senses are bereft. Wherefore, your poore subiects most
humble petition vnto your Highnesse is, that the lawes touching such malefactours,
may be put in due execution. For the whole of them is great, their doings horrible,
their malice intollerable, the examples most miserable. And I pray God, they
neuer practise further, then vpon the subiect. But this only by the way, these be
the scholers of Beelzebub the chiefe captaine of the Diuels" (Certaine Sermons,
1611, p. 204, in Workes of Jewell; cf. Parker Society edition, Part II, p. 1028). I
cannot date this sermon. 1572, the year to which it is assigned by Dr. Nicholson
(in his edition of Reginald Scot's Discouerie, p. xxxii), is certainly wrong, for Jewel
died in 1571. Strype associates it rather vaguely with the passage of the Witchcraft Act of 1563 (Annals of the Reformation, I, 8; cf. I, 295).

[206] Legge, The Scottish Review, XVIII, 262. See also Newes from Scotland
declaring the Damnable Life of Dr. Fian, 1591 (Roxburghe Club reprint).

when the Colony was just emerging from a political struggle that had threatened its very existence. For several years men's minds had been on the rack. The nervous condition of public feeling is wonderfully well depicted in a letter written in 1688 by the Rev. Joshua Moodey in Boston to Increase Mather, then in London as agent of the Colony. The Colonists are much pleased by the favor with which Mather has been received, but they distrust court promises. They are alarmed by a report that Mather and his associates have suffered "a great slurr" on account of certain over-zealous actions. Moodey rejoices in the death of Robert Mason, "one of the worst enemies that you & I & Mr. Morton had in these parts." Then there are the Indians:— "The cloud looks very dark and black upon us, & wee are under very awfull circumstances, which render an Indian Warr terrible to us." The Colonists shudder at a rumor that John Palmer, one of Andros's Council, is to come over as Supreme Judge, and know not how to reconcile it with the news of the progress their affairs have been making with the King. And finally, the writer gives an account of the case of Goodwin's afflicted children, which, as we know, was a kind of prologue to the Salem outbreak:— "Wee have a very strange th[ing] among us, which we know not what to make of, except it bee Witchcraft, as we think it must needs bee."[207] Clearly, there would have been small fear, in 1692, of a plot on Satan's part to destroy the Province, if our forefathers had not recently encountered other dangers of a more tangible kind.

In conclusion, I may venture to sum up, in the form of a number of brief theses, the main results at which we appear to have arrived in our discussion of witchcraft:—

1. The belief in witchcraft is the common heritage of humanity. It is not chargeable to any particular time, or race, or form of religion.

---

[207] Mather Papers, Mass. Hist. Soc. Collections, 4th Series, VIII, 366-368. This was the same Joshua Moodey, it will be remembered, who afterwards assisted Philip English and his family to escape from jail in Boston, and thus saved them from being executed as guilty of witchcraft (Sibley, Harvard Graduates, I, 376-377.)

2. Witchcraft in some shape or other is still credited by a majority of the human race.

3. The belief in witchcraft was practically universal in the seventeenth century, even among the educated; with the mass of the people it was absolutely universal.

4. To believe in witchcraft in the seventeenth century was no more discreditable to a man's head or heart than it was to believe in spontaneous generation or to be ignorant of the germ theory of disease.

5. The position of the seventeenth-century believers in witchcraft was logically and theologically stronger than that of the few persons who rejected the current belief.

6. The impulse to put a witch to death comes from the instinct of self-preservation. It is no more cruel or otherwise blameworthy, in itself, than the impulse to put a murderer to death.

7. The belief in witchcraft manifests itself, not in steady and continuous prosecution, but in sudden outbreaks occurring at irregular intervals.

8. Such outbreaks are not symptoms of extraordinary superstition or of a peculiarly acute state of unreason. They are due, like other panics, to a perturbed condition of the public mind. Hence they are likely to accompany, or to follow, crises in politics or religion.

9. The responsibility for any witch prosecution rests primarily on the community or neighborhood as a whole, not on the judge or the jury.

10. No jury, whether in a witch trial or in any other case, can be more enlightened than the general run of the vicinage.

11. Many persons who have been executed for witchcraft have supposed themselves to be guilty and have actually been guilty in intent.

12. Practically every person executed for witchcraft believed in the reality of such a crime, whether he supposed himself to be guilty of it or not.

13. The witch beliefs of New England were brought over from the Mother Country by the first settlers.

14. Spectral evidence had been admitted in the examinations and trials of witches in England for a hundred years before the Salem prosecutions took place.

15. Trials, convictions, and executions for witchcraft occurred in England after they had come to an end in Massachusetts, and they occurred on the Continent a hundred years later than that time.

16. Spectral evidence was admitted in English witch trials after such trials had ceased in Massachusetts.

17. The total number of persons executed for witchcraft in New England from the first settlement to the end of the century is inconsiderable, especially in view of what was going on in Europe.

18. The public repentance and recantation of judge and jury in Massachusetts have no parallel in the history of witchcraft.

19. The repentance and recantation came at a time which made them singularly effective arguments in the hands of the opponents of the witch dogma in England.

20. The record of New England in the matter of witchcraft is highly creditable, when considered as a whole and from the comparative point of view.

21. It is easy to be wise after the fact,—especially when the fact is two hundred years old.

CPSIA information can be obtained
at www.ICGtesting.com
Printed in the USA
LVOW11*1434130117

520894LV00007B/62/P

9 781162 046969